Computers Simplified™

— 3rd Edition —

IDG's 3-D Visual™ Series

IDG BOOKS *From* **maranGraphics™**

IDG Books Worldwide, Inc.
An International Data Group Company
Foster City, CA • Indianapolis • Chicago • Dallas

Computers Simplified™ 3rd Edition

Published by
IDG Books Worldwide, Inc.
An International Data Group Company
919 E. Hillsdale Blvd., Suite 400
Foster City, CA 94404
(415) 655-3000

Copyright© 1996 by maranGraphics Inc.
5755 Coopers Avenue
Mississauga, Ontario, Canada
L4Z 1R9

Library of Congress Catalog Card No.:
ISBN: 0-7645-6008-5
Printed in the United States of America
10 9 8 7 6 5 4 3 2

XX/XX/XX/XX/XX

Distributed in the United States by IDG Books Worldwide, Inc.
Distributed by Contemporanea de Ediciones for Venezuela; by Distribuidora Cuspide for Argentina; by CITEC for Brazil; by Ediciones ZETA S.C.R. Ltda. for Peru; by Editorial Limusa SA for Mexico; by Transworld Publishers Limited in the United Kingdom and Europe; by Academic Bookshop for Egypt; by Levant Distributors S.A.R.L. for Lebanon; by Al Jassim for Saudi Arabia; by Simron Pty. Ltd. for South Africa; by Pustak Mahal for India; by The Computer Bookshop for India; by Toppan Company Ltd. for Japan; by Addison Wesley Publishing Company for Korea; by Longman Singapore Publishers Ltd. for Singapore, Malaysia, Thailand, and Indonesia; by Unalis Corporation for Taiwan; by WS Computer Publishing Company, Inc. for the Philippines; by WoodsLane Pty. Ltd. for Australia; by WoodsLane Enterprises Ltd. for New Zealand. Authorized Sales Agent: Anthony Rudkin Associates for the Middle East and North Africa.

For general information on IDG Books Worldwide's books in the U.S., please call our Consumer Customer Service department at 800-762-2974. For reseller information, including discounts and premium sales, please call our Reseller Customer Service department at 800-434-3422.

For information on where to purchase IDG Books Worldwide's books outside the U.S., please contact our International Sales department at 415-655-3172 or fax 415-655-3295.

For information on foreign language translations, please contact our Foreign & Subsidiary Rights department at 415-655-3021 or fax 415-655-3281.

For U.S. Corporate Sales and quantity discounts, contact maranGraphics at 800-469-6616.

For sales inquiries and special prices for bulk quantities, please contact our Sales department at 415-655-3200.

For authorization to photocopy items for corporate, personal, or educational use, please contact maranGraphics Inc., 5755 Coopers Avenue, Mississauga, Ontario, L4Z 1R9, or fax (905) 890-9434.

For information on using IDG Books Worldwide's books in the classroom or for ordering examination copies, please contact our Educational Sales department at 1-800-434-2086 or fax 817-251-8174.

Trademark Acknowledgments

©1996
maranGraphics, Inc.

The animated characters are the copyright of maranGraphics, Inc.

U.S. Corporate Sales	**U.S. Trade Sales**
Contact maranGraphics at (800) 469-6616 or Fax (905) 890-9434.	Contact IDG Books at (800) 434-3422 or (415) 655-3000.

Welcome to the world of IDG Books Worldwide.

IDG Books Worldwide, Inc., is a subsidiary of International Data Group, the world's largest publisher of computer-related information and the leading global provider of information services on information technology. IDG was founded more than 25 years ago and now employs more than 8,500 people worldwide. IDG publishes more than 270 computer publications in over 75 countries (see listing below). More than 90 million people read one or more IDG publications each month.

Launched in 1990, IDG Books Worldwide is today the #1 publisher of best-selling computer books in the United States. We are proud to have received eight awards from the Computer Press Association in recognition of editorial excellence and three from Computer Currents' First Annual Readers' Choice Awards. Our best-selling ...For Dummies® series has more than 25 million copies in print with translations in 30 languages. IDG Books Worldwide, through a joint venture with IDG's Hi-Tech Beijing, became the first U.S. publisher to publish a computer book in the People's Republic of China. In record time, IDG Books Worldwide has become the first choice for millions of readers around the world who want to learn how to better manage their businesses.

Our mission is simple: Every one of our books is designed to bring extra value and skill-building instructions to the reader. Our books are written by experts who understand and care about our readers. The knowledge base of our editorial staff comes from years of experience in publishing, education, and journalism - experience which we use to produce books for the '90s. In short, we care about books, so we attract the best people. We devote special attention to details such as audience, interior design, use of icons, and illustrations. And because we use an efficient process of authoring, editing, and desktop publishing our books electronically, we can spend more time ensuring superior content and spend less time on the technicalities of making books.

You can count on our commitment to deliver high-quality books at competitive prices on topics you want to read about. At IDG Books Worldwide, we continue in the IDG tradition of delivering quality for more than 25 years. You'll find no better book on a subject than one from IDG Books Worldwide.

John Kilcullen
President and CEO
IDG Books Worldwide, Inc.

*Every maranGraphics book represents
the extraordinary vision and commitment of a unique family:
the Maran family of Toronto, Canada.*

Back Row (from left to right): Sherry Maran, Rob Maran, Richard Maran, Maxine Maran, Jill Maran.
Front Row (from left to right): Judy Maran, Ruth Maran.

Richard Maran is the company founder and its inspirational leader. He developed maranGraphics' proprietary communication technology called "visual grammar." This book is built on that technology—empowering readers with the easiest and quickest way to learn about computers.

Ruth Maran is the Author and Architect—a role Richard established that now bears Ruth's distinctive touch. She creates the words and visual structure that are the basis for the books.

Judy Maran is the Project Manager. She works with Ruth, Richard, and the highly talented maranGraphics illustrators, designers, and editors to transform Ruth's material into its final form.

Rob Maran is the Technical and Production Specialist. He makes sure the state-of-the-art technology used to create these books always performs as it should.

Sherry Maran manages the Reception, Order Desk, and any number of areas that require immediate attention and a helping hand.

Jill Maran is a jack-of-all-trades and dynamo who fills in anywhere she's needed anytime she's back from university.

Maxine Maran is the Business Manager and family sage. She maintains order in the business and family—and keeps everything running smoothly.

Oh, and three other family members are seated on the sofa. These graphic disk characters help make it fun and easy to learn about computers. They're part of the extended maranGraphics family.

Credits

Author and Architect:
Ruth Maran

Technical Reviewers:
Paul Whitehead
Maarten Heilbron

Technical Consultant (Macintosh Chapter):
Ian Campbell

Copy Development (Macintosh Chapter):
Alison MacAlpine

Restructuring of Chapters & Indexer:
Kelleigh Wing

Project Manager:
Judy Maran

Editors:
Susan Beytas
Karen Derrah

Layout Design & Ilustrations:
Tamara Poliquin

Illustrators:
Chris K.C. Leung
Russell Marini
Noel Clannon
Andrew Trowbridge
Julie Lane

Screen Shot Permissions:
Sherry Maran

Post Production & Technical Reviewer (Macintosh Chapter):
Robert Maran

Acknowledgments

Thanks to the dedicated staff of maranGraphics, including Susan Beytas, Noel Clannon, Karen Derrah, Francisco Ferreira, Brad Hilderley, Chris K.C. Leung, Alison MacAlpine, Jill Maran, Judy Maran, Maxine Maran, Robert Maran, Sherry Maran, Russ Marini, Tamara Poliquin, Christie Van Duin, Paul Whitehead and Kelleigh Wing.

Finally, to Richard Maran who originated the easy-to-use graphic format of this guide. Thank you for your inspiration and guidance.

Screen Shot Permissions

Screens That Appear Throughout The Book

Apple, the Apple logo and the Macintosh computer and screen copyright Apple Computer, Inc. Used with permission.

Dell computer logo used with permission from Dell Corporation.

Intel chips used with permission. Intel486SX™, Intel486DX™, Intel486DX2™, Intel486DX4™, Intel 150 MHz Pentium®, Intel 200 MHz Pentium®, Intel Pentium® Pro and OverDrive® are registered trademarks of Intel Corporation.

Microsoft Windows 95, Microsoft Excel for Windows 95, Microsoft Word for Windows 95, Microsoft Excel 5, Microsoft Word 6 and Microsoft PowerPoint for Windows 3.1 screen shots reprinted by permission from Microsoft Corporation. Microsoft, Windows and PowerPoint are registered trademarks.

Netscape screen shots used with permission. Netscape and Netscape Navigator are trademarks of Netscape Communications Corp.

Chapter 2

ENERGY STAR logo and screen reprinted with permission from Environmental Protection Agency (EPA).

Lotus 1-2-3 Release 5 screen shots © 1996 Lotus Development Corporation. Used with permission of Lotus Development Corporation. Lotus and 1-2-3 are registered trademarks of Lotus Development Corporation.

Chapter 3

AMD chip copyright © 1995 Advanced Micro Devices, Inc. Reprinted with permission of copyright owner. All other rights reserved. AMD, the AMD logo, Am5x86, and 5x86 are trademarks of Advanced Micro Devices, Inc. and may not be used in advertising or publicity pertaining to distribution of this information without specific, written prior permission.

Cyrix chip used with permission. Cyrix Corporation, (http://www.cyrix.com), headquartered in Richardson, Texas, is a leading supplier of high-performance processors and systems to the personal computer industry. Founded in 1988, the company designs, manufactures and markets innovative x86 software-compatible processors for the desktop and mobile computer markets. The Cyrix 6x86 processor was recently recognized for its performance with awards from a number of publications, including Byte Magazine's Best Technology at CeBIT '96, PC Week's Corporate IT Excellence Award and Windows Sources' Stellar Award.

Chapter 4

Grammar Rock screen shot used with permission from Creative Wonders. Screen shot used on page 88.

Iomega Zip drive used with permission from Iomega Corporation.

Mavis Beacon Teaches Typing screen shot reprinted with permission from Mindscape, Inc.

Microsoft® screen shots of Microsoft Golf, Microsoft Musical Instruments and Microsoft Dinosaurs reprinted with permission from Microsoft Corporation. Images from Dorling Kindersley.

Windows® 3.1 Write screen shot reprinted by permission from Microsoft Corporation.

Chapter 6

Microsoft® Access for Windows® 95 screen shot reprinted by permission from Microsoft Corporation.

Microsoft® box shot of Microsoft Office Packaged Product reprinted with permission from Microsoft Corporation. Microsoft Office logo (puzzle design) is a trademark of Microsoft Corporation.

Chapter 7

Microsoft® MS-DOS, Windows® 3.1 and Windows for Workgroups 3.11 screen shots reprinted by permission from Microsoft Corporation. MS-DOS is a registered trademark.

Chapter 8

Microsoft® Excel for the Macintosh screen shot reprinted by permission from Microsoft Corporation.

Motorola chips used with permission from Motorola, Inc.

Chapter 10

CompuServe screen shot reprinted with permission. CompuServe is a registered trademark of CompuServe Incorporated.

USA TODAY Online screen shot used with permission. Copyright 1996 USA TODAY Online.

Chapter 12

AltaVista screen shot reprinted with permission. AltaVista and the AltaVista logo are trademarks and service marks of Digital Equipment Corporation.

Complete Works of William Shakespeare screen shot reprinted with permission.

Empire Mall screen shot reprinted with permission.

Flower Stop screen shot reprinted with permission. http://www.flowerstop.com

Infoseek screen shot reprinted by permission. Infoseek, Infoseek Guide, Infoseek Personal and the Infoseek logo are trademarks of Infoseek Corporation which may be registered in certain jurisdictions. Copyright © 1995, 1996 Infoseek Corporation. All rights reserved.

Le Grand Louvre Mona Lisa screen shot reprinted with permission.

Sound Spectrum screen shot reprinted with permission.

Yahoo screen shot reprinted with permission. Text and artwork copyright © 1996 by YAHOO!, Inc. All rights reserved. YAHOO! and the YAHOO! logo are trademarks of YAHOO!, Inc.

Chapter 13

ArchiePlexForm screen shot reprinted by permission from NASA Lewis Research Center.

Library of Congress screen (from their FTP site) used with permission from the Library of Congress.

Shareware.com screen shot reprinted with permission from CNET: The Computer Network, copyright 1996.

TABLE OF CONTENTS

TABLE OF CONTENTS

TABLE OF CONTENTS

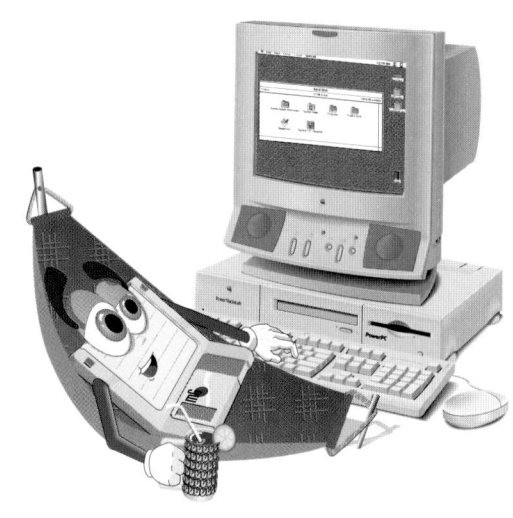

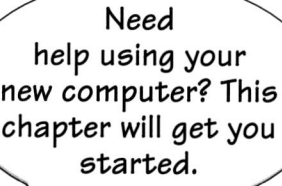

Need help using your new computer? This chapter will get you started.

INTRODUCTION TO COMPUTERS

HARDWARE AND SOFTWARE

HARDWARE

Hardware is any part of a computer system you can see or touch.

Hardware and software are the two basic parts of a computer system.

Peripheral

A peripheral is any piece of hardware attached to a computer, such as a printer.

SOFTWARE

Software is a set of electronic instructions that tell a computer what to do. You cannot see or touch software, but you can see and touch the packaging the software comes in.

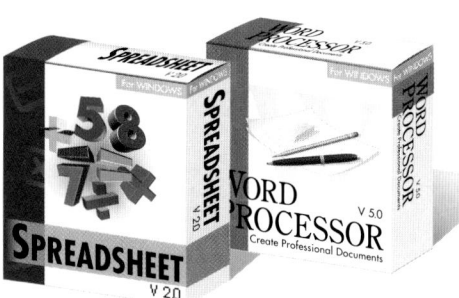

Application Software

Application software lets you accomplish specific tasks. Popular application software includes Microsoft® Word and Lotus 1-2-3.

Operating System Software

Operating system software controls the overall activity of a computer. Most new computers come with the Windows 95 operating system software.

GETTING HELP

> There are many ways to get help when using new hardware and software.

Documentation

Hardware and software should come with printed documentation that tells you how to set up and use the product. Many software packages also come with a built-in help feature. You can also check local book stores for manuals with detailed, step-by-step instructions.

Call the Experts

If you have questions about setting up or using new hardware or software, try calling the store where you purchased the product.

Classes

Colleges and computer stores often offer computer courses. Many communities also have computer clubs where you can ask questions and exchange ideas.

HOW COMPUTERS WORK

> A computer collects, processes, stores and outputs information.

INPUT

An input device lets you communicate with a computer. You can use input devices to enter information and issue commands. A keyboard, mouse and joystick are input devices.

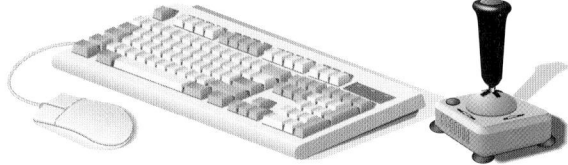

PROCESS

The Central Processing Unit (CPU) is the main chip in a computer. The CPU processes instructions, performs calculations and manages the flow of information through a computer system. The CPU communicates with input, output and storage devices to perform tasks.

STORE

A storage device holds information. The computer uses information stored on these devices to perform tasks. A hard drive, tape drive, floppy disk and CD-ROM drive are storage devices.

OUTPUT

An output device lets a computer communicate with you. These devices display information on a screen, create printed copies or generate sound. A monitor, printer and speakers are output devices.

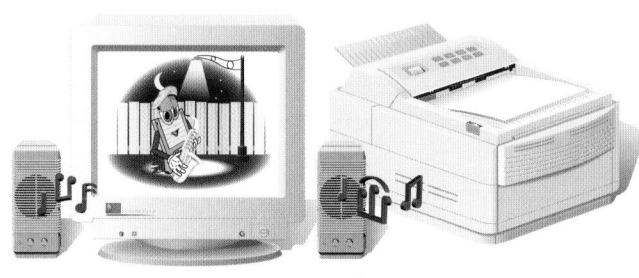

BYTES

> Bytes are used to measure the amount of information a device can store.

Byte

One byte is one character. A character can be a number, letter or symbol.

One byte consists of eight bits (binary digits). A bit is the smallest unit of information a computer can process.

Kilobyte (K)

One kilobyte is 1,024 characters. This is approximately equal to one page of double-spaced text.

Megabyte (MB)

One megabyte is 1,048,576 characters. This is approximately equal to one novel.

Gigabyte (GB)

One gigabyte is 1,073,741,824 characters. This is approximately equal to one thousand novels.

TYPES OF COMPUTER SYSTEMS

> There are several types of computer systems.

PC (PERSONAL COMPUTER)

A PC is a computer designed to meet the needs of a single person and usually refers to IBM-compatible computers. PCs are found in many businesses and are popular for home use.

MACINTOSH

Macintosh computers are found in many homes and are very popular in the graphics, publishing and multimedia industries. The Macintosh was the first widely used computer that offered a graphical display.

MAINFRAME

A mainframe is a computer that can process and store large amounts of information and support many users at the same time. Mainframes are often used by banks and insurance companies.

Mainframes process and store information entered on terminals. A terminal consists of a keyboard and monitor and is only used to input and output information.

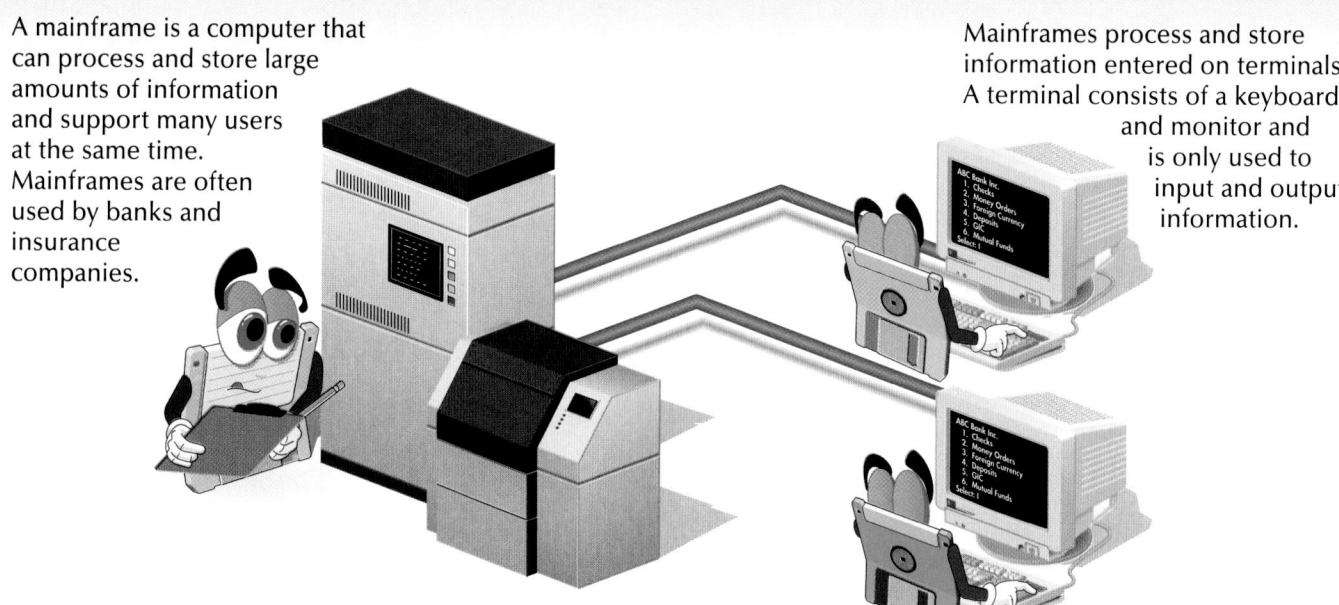

A TYPICAL COMPUTER

A typical computer system consists of several parts.

Monitor

A monitor is a device that displays text and images generated by the computer.

Computer Case

A computer case contains all the major components of a computer system.

Printer

A printer is a device that produces a paper copy of documents you create on the computer.

Modem

A modem is a device that lets computers communicate through telephone lines. A modem can be found inside or outside the computer case.

Keyboard

A keyboard is a device that lets you type information and instructions into a computer.

Mouse

A mouse is a hand-held device that lets you select and move items on the screen.

INSIDE A COMPUTER

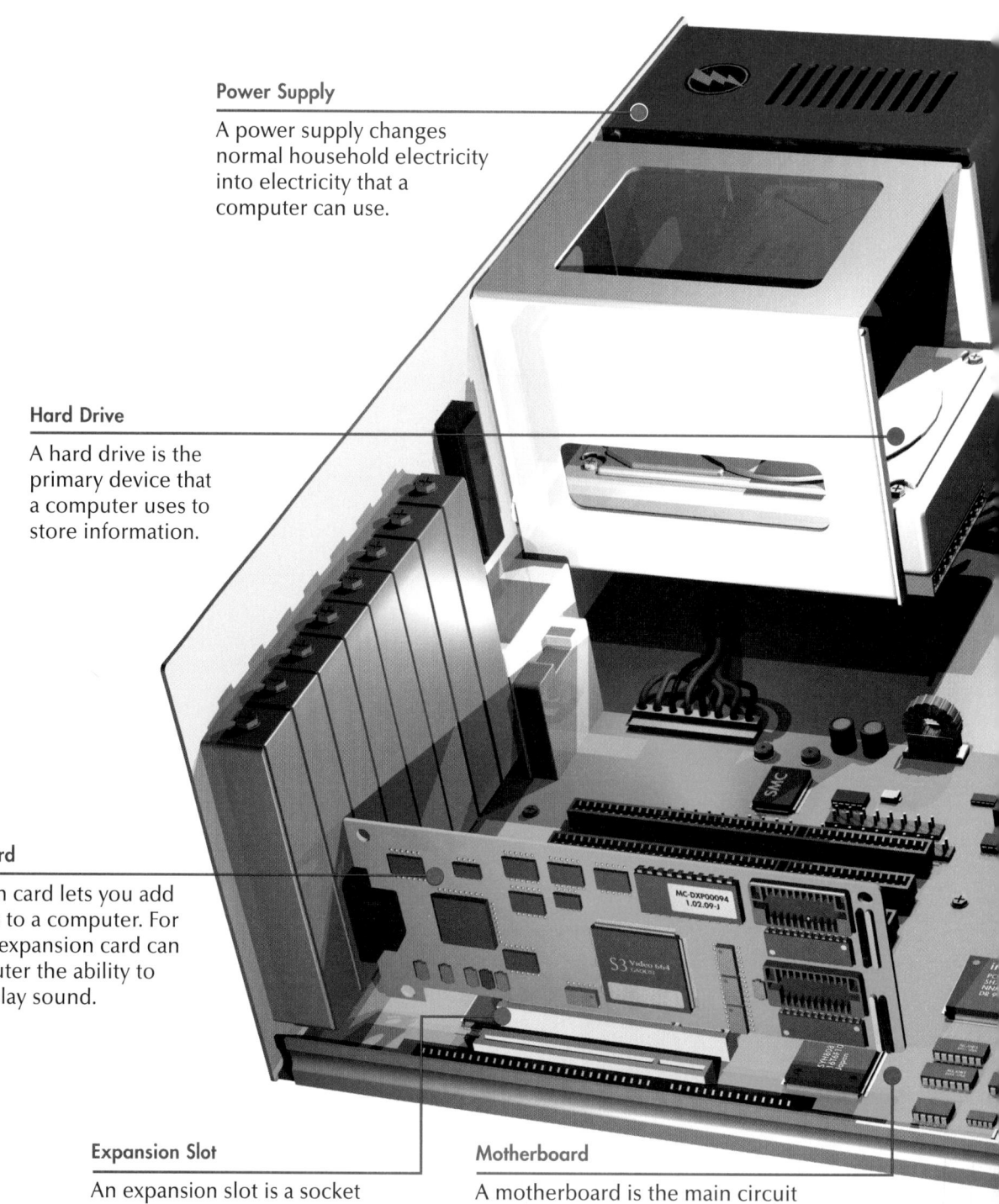

Power Supply

A power supply changes normal household electricity into electricity that a computer can use.

Hard Drive

A hard drive is the primary device that a computer uses to store information.

Expansion Card

An expansion card lets you add new features to a computer. For example, an expansion card can give a computer the ability to record and play sound.

Expansion Slot

An expansion slot is a socket on the motherboard. An expansion card plugs into an expansion slot.

Motherboard

A motherboard is the main circuit board of a computer. All electrical components plug into the motherboard.

All computers contain the same basic components.

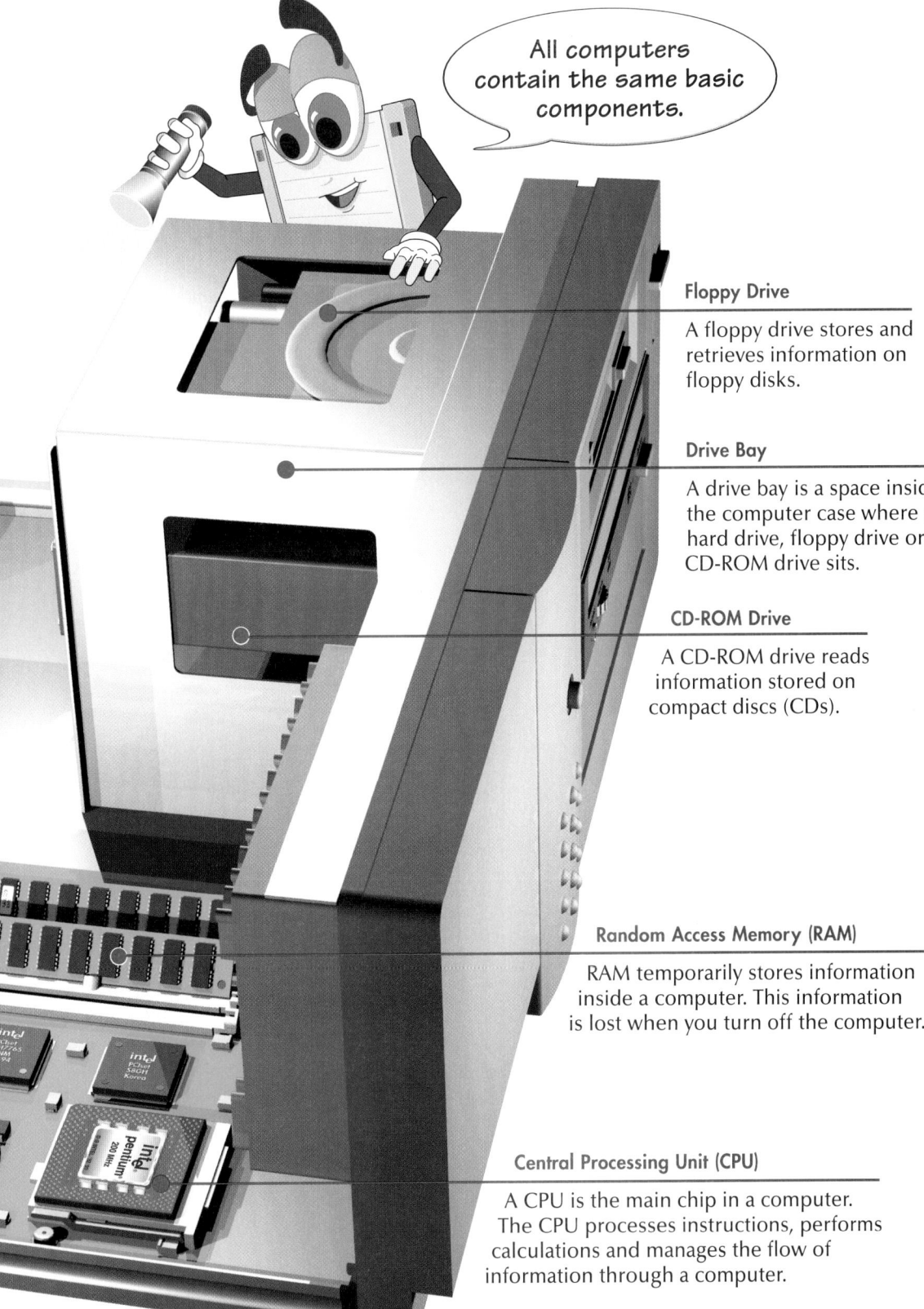

Floppy Drive

A floppy drive stores and retrieves information on floppy disks.

Drive Bay

A drive bay is a space inside the computer case where a hard drive, floppy drive or CD-ROM drive sits.

CD-ROM Drive

A CD-ROM drive reads information stored on compact discs (CDs).

Random Access Memory (RAM)

RAM temporarily stores information inside a computer. This information is lost when you turn off the computer.

Central Processing Unit (CPU)

A CPU is the main chip in a computer. The CPU processes instructions, performs calculations and manages the flow of information through a computer.

COMPUTER CASE

A computer case contains all the major components of a computer system.

Desktop Case

A desktop case usually sits on a desk, under a monitor.

Tower Case

A tower case usually sits on the floor. This provides more desk space, but can be less convenient for inserting and removing floppy disks and CD-ROM discs.

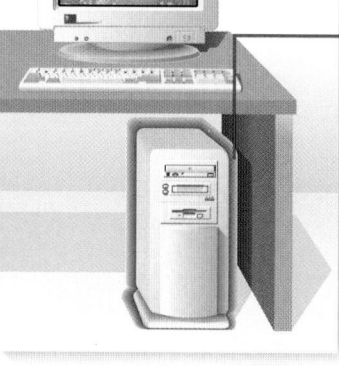

PORTABLE

A portable is a small, lightweight computer that you can easily transport. A portable has a built-in keyboard and screen.

ALL-IN-ONE CASE

An all-in-one case contains a monitor, disk drive, CD-ROM drive and speakers in a single unit.

POWER SUPPLY

A power supply changes the alternating current (AC) that comes from an outlet to the direct current (DC) that a computer can use.

The capacity of a power supply is measured in watts. An average computer uses up to 200 watts, whereas an average light bulb uses 60 watts.

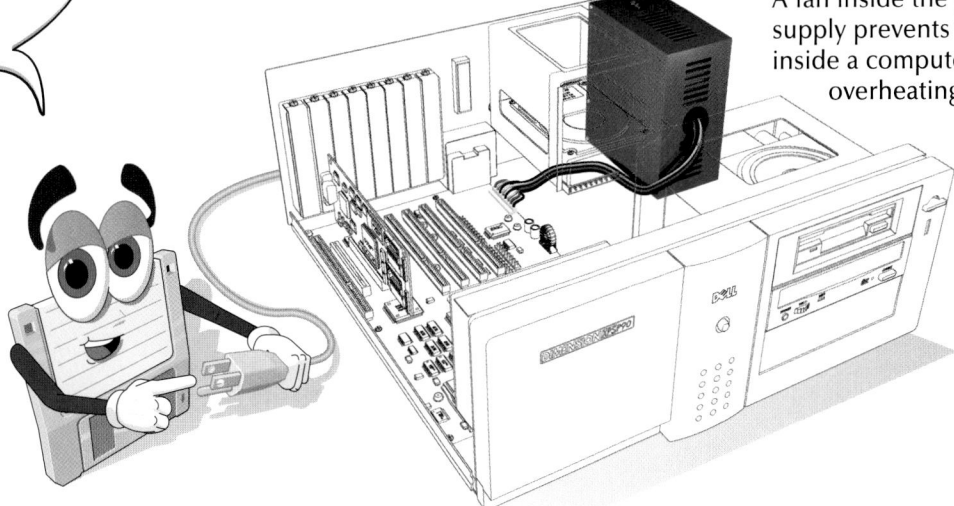

A fan inside the power supply prevents the parts inside a computer from overheating.

PROTECT YOUR EQUIPMENT

Changes in electrical power can damage equipment and information.

Surge Protector

A surge protector, or surge suppressor, guards a computer against surges. A surge is a fluctuation in power. These fluctuations happen most often during storms.

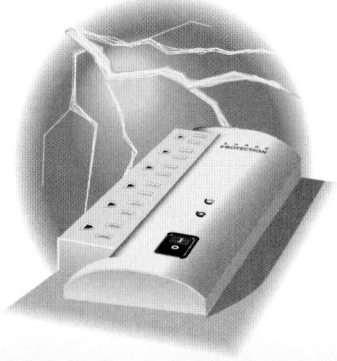

UPS

An Uninterruptible Power Supply (UPS) protects a computer from a loss of power. A UPS contains a battery that stores electrical power. If the power fails, the battery can run the computer for a short time so you can save your information.

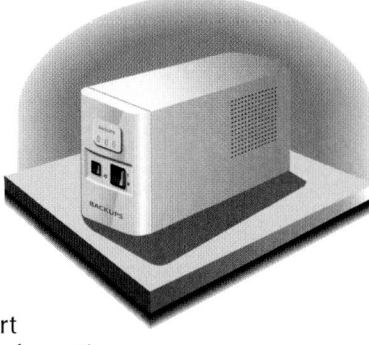

> A port is a connector at the back of a computer where you plug in an external device such as a printer or modem. This allows instructions and data to flow between the computer and the device.

Parallel Port

A parallel port has 25 holes. This type of port is known as a female connector. A parallel port connects a printer or tape drive.

A computer internally labels each parallel port with the letters LPT. The first parallel port is named LPT1, the second parallel port is named LPT2, and so on.

Monitor Port

A monitor port connects a monitor.

Serial Port

A serial port has either 9 or 25 pins. This type of port is known as a male connector. A serial port connects a mouse or modem.

A computer internally labels each serial port with the letters COM. The first serial port is named COM1, the second serial port is named COM2, and so on.

Keyboard Port

A keyboard port connects a keyboard.

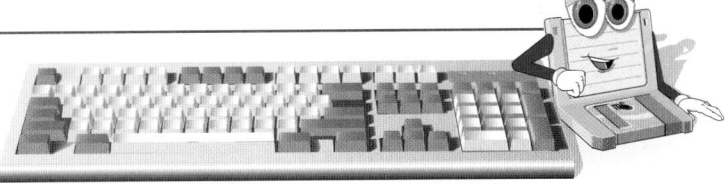

Game Port

A game port connects a joystick.

NEW!

USB

Universal Serial Bus (USB) is a new type of port that provides a way to connect multiple devices using only one port. For example, you can connect a printer, modem, joystick and scanner to a single USB port.

EXPANSION CARD

> An expansion card is a circuit board that lets you add a new feature to a computer.

An expansion card is also called an expansion board.

EXPANSION SLOT

An expansion slot is a socket where you plug in an expansion card.

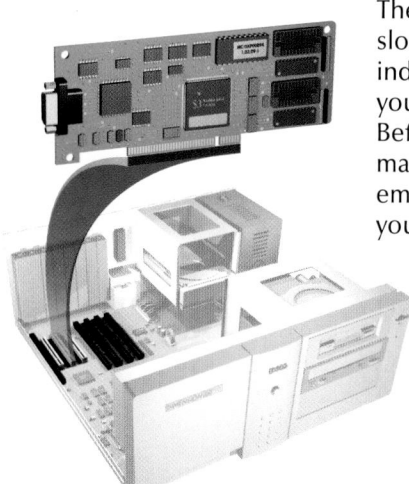

The number of expansion slots your computer has indicates how many features you can add to the computer. Before you buy a computer, make sure it has enough empty expansion slots for your future needs.

CONNECT DEVICES

Some expansion cards are accessible from the back of a computer. These expansion cards contain ports where you can plug in devices. For example, you can plug speakers into a sound card to hear the sound generated by the computer.

TYPES OF EXPANSION CARDS

A computer usually comes with one or more expansion cards.

Video

A video card generates the images displayed on the monitor.

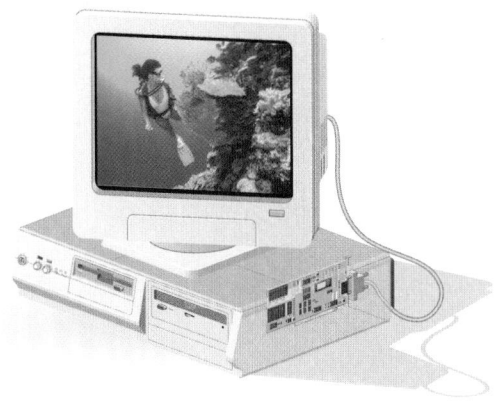

Modem

A modem card lets computers exchange information through telephone lines.

Sound

A sound card lets a computer play and record high-quality sound.

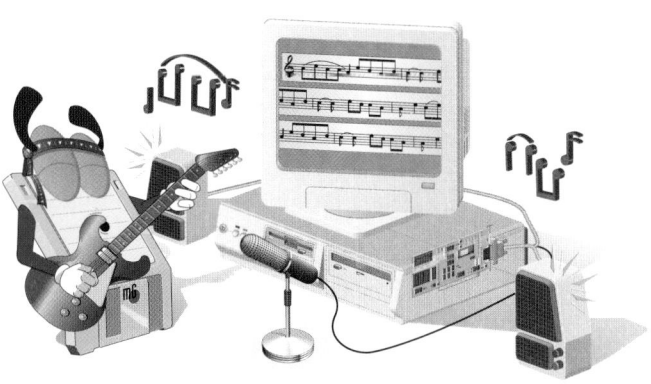

Networking

A network interface card lets connected computers share information and equipment.

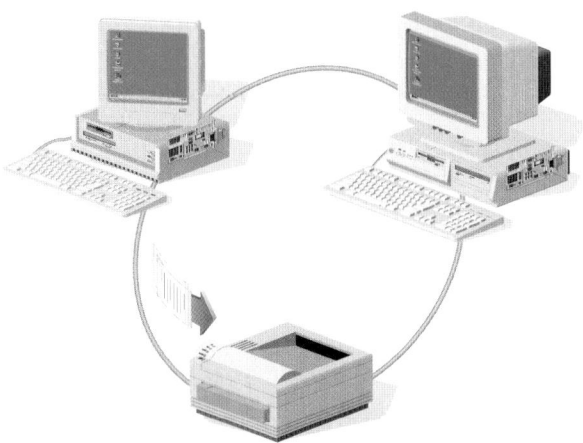

INPUT AND OUTPUT

MOUSE

A mouse is a hand-held pointing device that lets you select and move items on your screen.

A mouse can come in various shapes, colors and sizes.

USE THE MOUSE

Resting your hand on the mouse, use your thumb and two rightmost fingers to move the mouse on the desk. Use your two remaining fingers to press the mouse buttons.

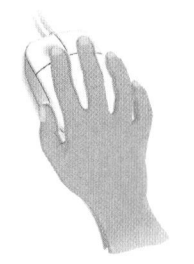

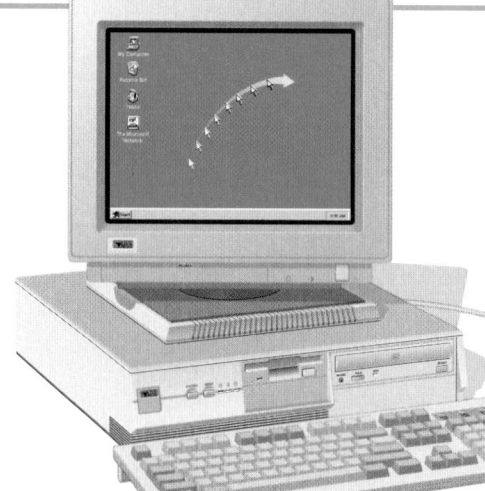

When you move the mouse on your desk, the pointer on the screen moves in the same direction. The pointer assumes different shapes (example: $\mathbb{k}$ or I) depending on its location on the screen and the task you are performing.

MOUSE ACTIONS

There are four common mouse actions.

Click

A click often selects an item on the screen. To click, press and release the left mouse button.

Drag and Drop

Dragging and dropping makes it easy to move an item on the screen. Position the pointer over an item on the screen and then press and hold down the left mouse button. Still holding down the button, move the pointer to where you want to place the item and then release the button.

Double-Click

A double-click often opens a document or starts a program. To double-click, quickly press and release the left mouse button twice.

Right-Click

A right-click often displays a list of commands on the screen. To right-click, press and release the right mouse button.

LEFT-HANDED USERS

If you are left-handed, you can switch the functions of the left and right mouse buttons to make the mouse easier to use. For example, to click an item, you would press the right button instead of the left.

MOUSE continued

MOUSE PAD

Hard plastic mouse pads tend to attract less dirt and provide a smoother surface than fabric-covered mouse pads.

> A mouse pad provides a smooth surface for moving a mouse and reduces the amount of dirt that enters the mouse.

You can buy mouse pads displaying interesting designs or pictures at most computer stores. Some mouse pads have built-in wrist support for increased comfort.

CLEAN THE MOUSE

You should occasionally remove and clean the ball inside the mouse. Make sure you also remove dust and dirt from the inside to help ensure smooth motion of the mouse.

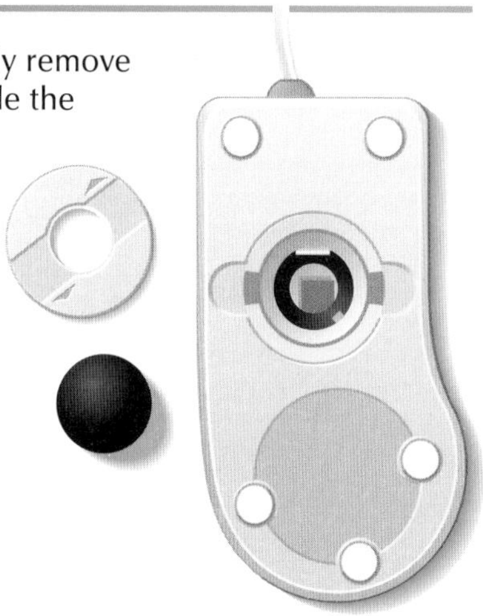

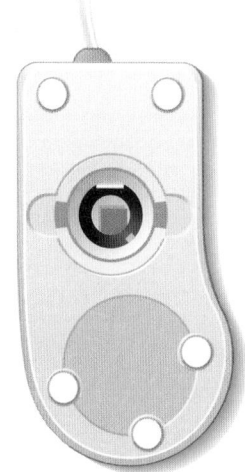

CORDLESS MOUSE

A cordless mouse runs on a battery and reduces the clutter on your desk by eliminating the mouse cord. When you move the mouse on your desk, the mouse sends signals through the air to your computer, the same way a remote control sends signals to a television.

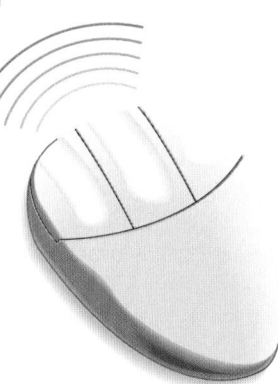

OTHER POINTING DEVICES

Joystick

A joystick helps you control the movement of people and objects in many computer games. Joysticks are used for arcade-type computer games because they let you move quickly and accurately in any direction.

Touchpad

A touchpad is a surface that is sensitive to pressure and motion. When you move your fingertip across the pad, the pointer on the screen moves in the same direction.

Trackball

A trackball is an upside-down mouse that remains stationary on your desk. You roll the ball with your fingers or palm to move the pointer on the screen. A trackball is a great alternative to a mouse when you have limited desk space.

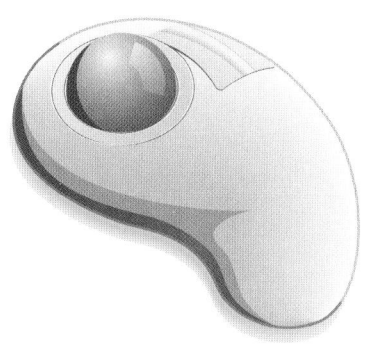

KEYBOARD

The keys on a keyboard let you enter information and instructions into a computer.

Most keyboards have 101 keys. Your keyboard may look different from the keyboard shown here.

Function Keys

These keys let you quickly perform specific tasks. For example, in many programs you can press **F1** to display help information.

Escape Key

You can press **Esc** to quit a task you are performing.

Caps Lock and Shift Keys

These keys let you enter text in uppercase (ABC) and lowercase (abc) letters.

Press **Caps Lock** to change the case of all letters you type. Press the key again to return to the original case.

Press **Shift** in combination with another key to type an uppercase letter.

Ctrl and Alt Keys

You can use the **Ctrl** or **Alt** key in combination with another key to perform a specific task. For example, in some programs you can press **Ctrl** and **S** to save a document.

Spacebar

You can press the **Spacebar** to insert a blank space.

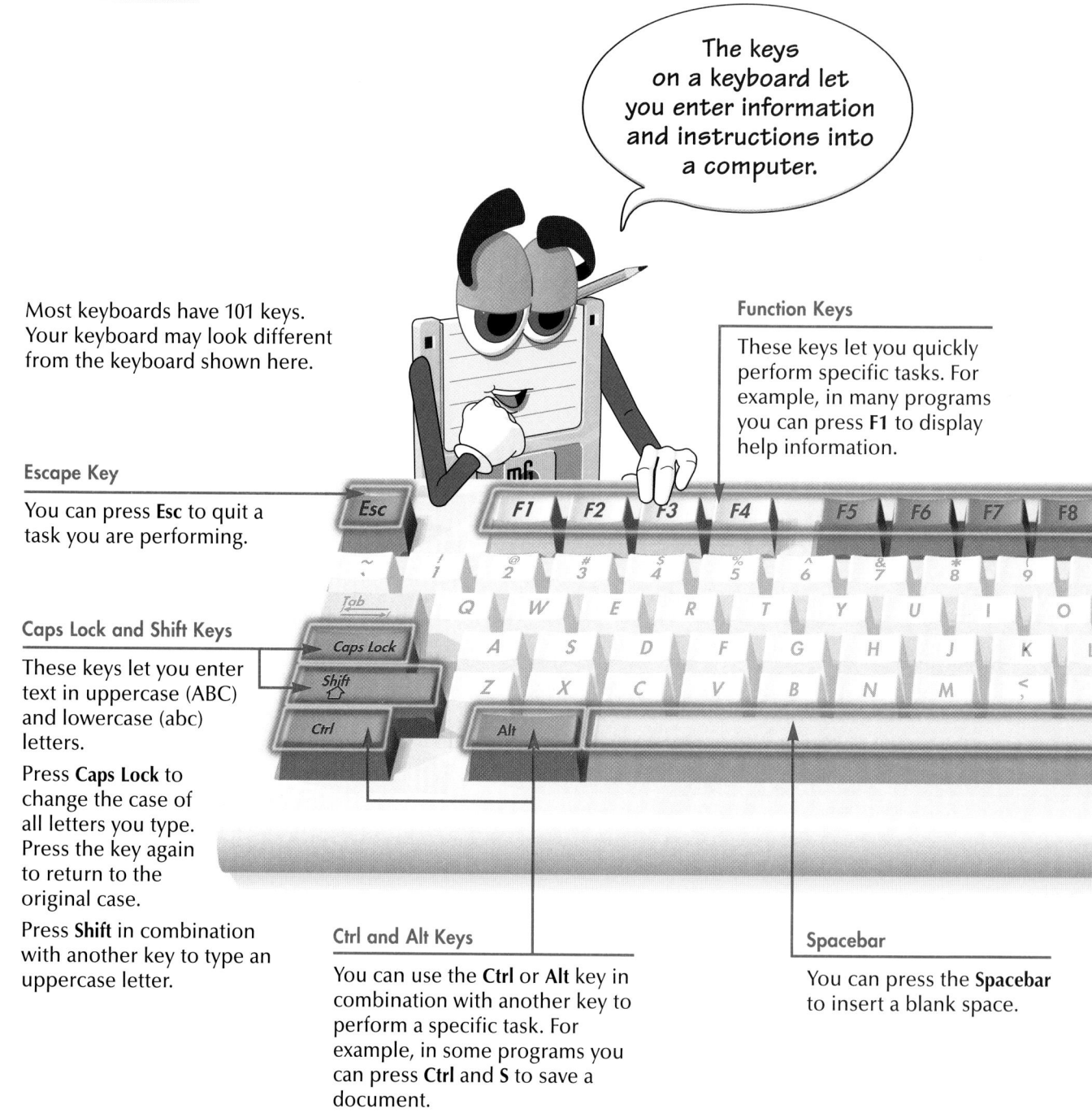

Backspace Key

You can press **Backspace** to remove the character to the left of the cursor.

Delete Key

You can press **Delete** to remove the character to the right of the cursor.

Status Lights

These lights indicate whether the **Num Lock** or **Caps Lock** features are on or off.

Numeric Keypad

When the **Num Lock** light is on, you can use the number keys (0 through 9) to enter numbers. When the **Num Lock** light is off, you can use these keys to move the cursor around the screen. To turn the light on or off, press **Num Lock**.

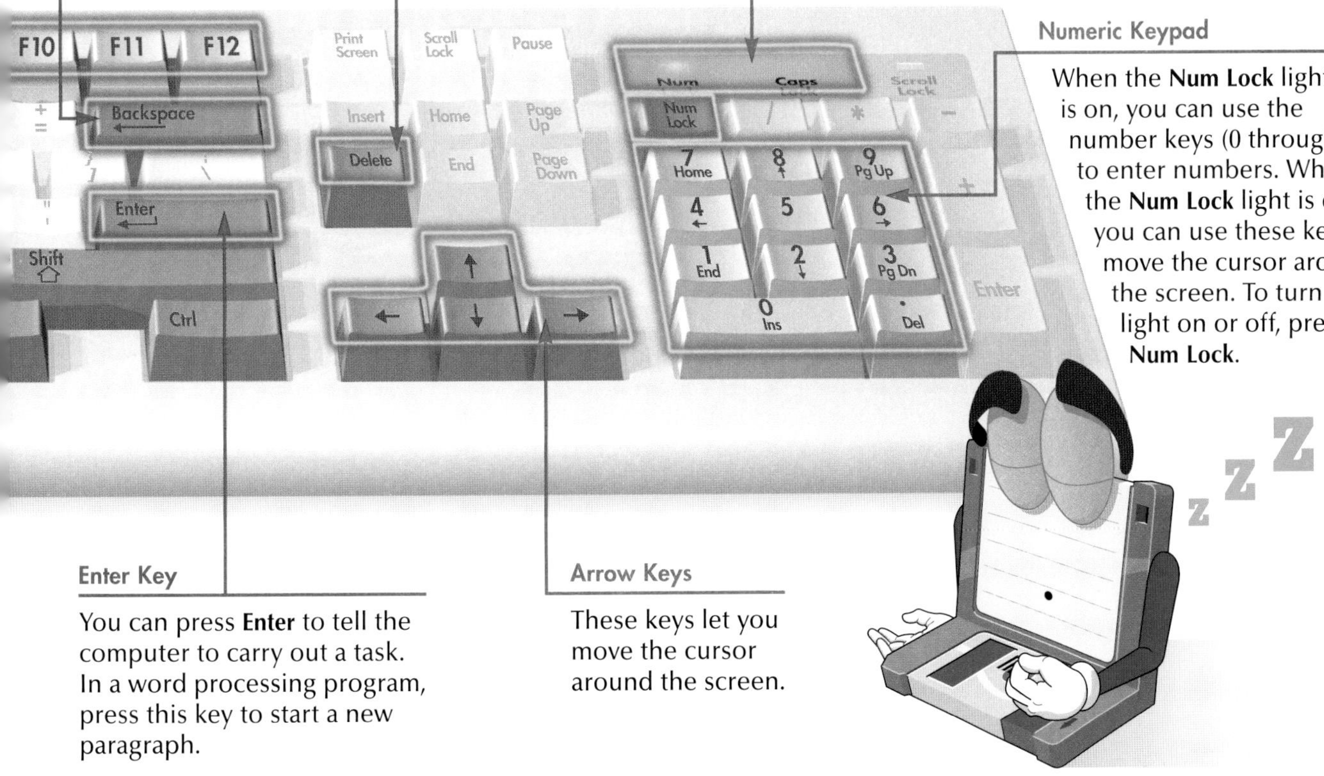

Enter Key

You can press **Enter** to tell the computer to carry out a task. In a word processing program, press this key to start a new paragraph.

Arrow Keys

These keys let you move the cursor around the screen.

PRINTER

A printer produces a paper copy of the information displayed on the screen.

You can buy a printer that produces black-and-white or color images.

You can use a printer to produce letters, invoices, newsletters, transparencies, labels, packing slips and much more.

CHOOSE A PRINTER

There are several factors to consider when buying a printer.

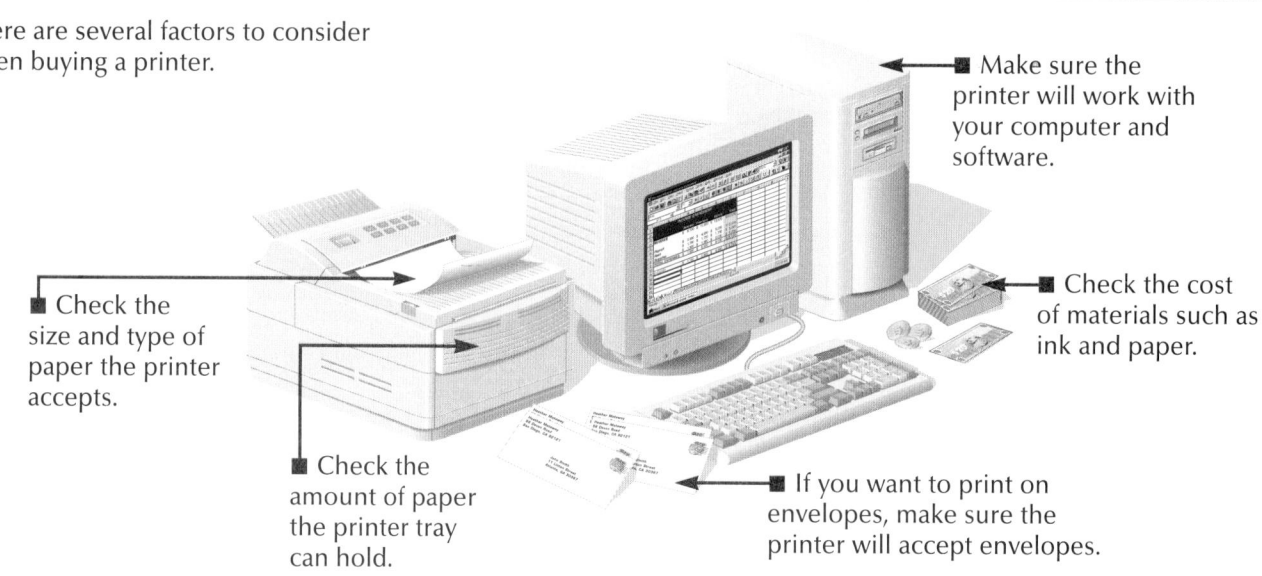

■ Make sure the printer will work with your computer and software.

■ Check the cost of materials such as ink and paper.

■ Check the size and type of paper the printer accepts.

■ Check the amount of paper the printer tray can hold.

■ If you want to print on envelopes, make sure the printer will accept envelopes.

PRINTER SPEED

The speed of a printer determines how quickly it can print the pages you selected. Speed is measured in characters per second (cps) or pages per minute (ppm). A higher speed results in faster output.

A complicated page, such as a page that contains graphics, takes longer to print than a page that contains only text.

PRINTER RESOLUTION

The resolution of a printer determines the quality of the images it can produce. A higher resolution results in sharper, more detailed images.

Printer resolution is measured in dots per inch (dpi). Generally, a resolution of 300 dpi is acceptable for most office documents, although 600 dpi printers are becoming the standard.

300 dpi   600 dpi   1200 dpi

DOT-MATRIX PRINTER

A dot-matrix printer is the least expensive type of printer. This type of printer works by impact.

Inside a dot-matrix printer, a print head containing small, blunt pins strikes an inked ribbon. This striking action makes a dot-matrix printer quite loud.

Speed

Most dot-matrix printers produce images at a speed of 25 to 450 characters per second (cps) or 1 to 18 pages per minute (ppm).

Resolution

The resolution, or quality, of the images produced by a dot-matrix printer depends on the number of pins in the print head.

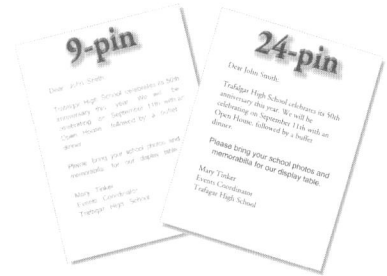

You can buy a 9-pin or 24-pin dot-matrix printer. A 9-pin dot-matrix printer produces draft-quality documents. A 24-pin printer produces typewriter-quality documents.

Ink

Dot-matrix printers store ink on ribbons similar to typewriter ribbons. When the ink runs out, you replace the ribbon.

Paper

A dot-matrix printer typically uses continuous form paper. This paper has holes punched along each side and connects from end to end.

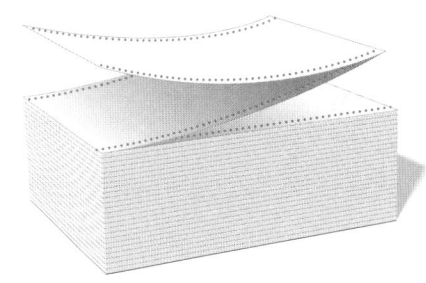

Narrow or Wide Carriage

You can buy either a narrow carriage or wide carriage dot-matrix printer. A narrow carriage printer accepts 8 1/2 by 11-inch paper. A wide carriage printer accepts many different paper sizes.

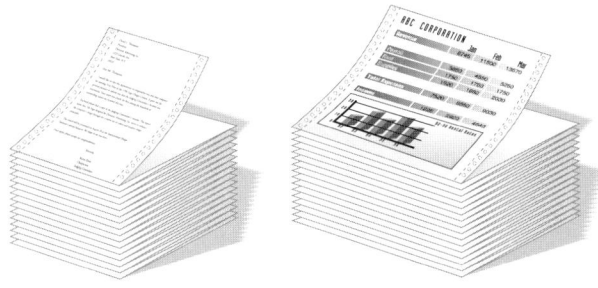

Multipart Forms

A dot-matrix printer is ideal for printing on multipart forms, which need an impact to print through multiple copies. Stores and courier companies frequently use multipart forms to print receipts.

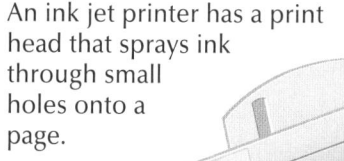

INK JET PRINTER

An ink jet printer has a print head that sprays ink through small holes onto a page.

An ink jet printer produces high-quality documents at a relatively low price. This type of printer is ideal for routine business and personal documents.

Ink jet printers and Bubble Jet printers work the same way.

Speed

Most ink jet printers produce images at a speed of 0.5 to 4 pages per minute (ppm).

Resolution

The resolution, or quality, of the images produced by an ink jet printer ranges from 180 to 720 dots per inch (dpi).

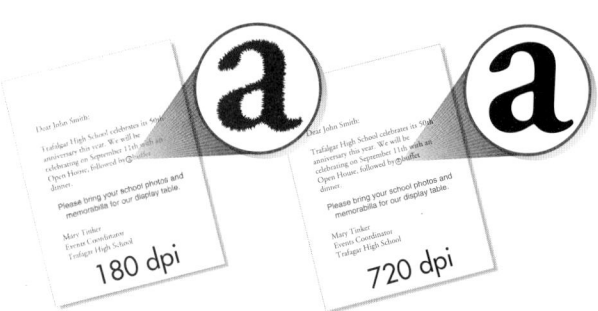

Ink

Ink jet printers use ink stored in cartridges. When the ink runs out, you replace the cartridge.

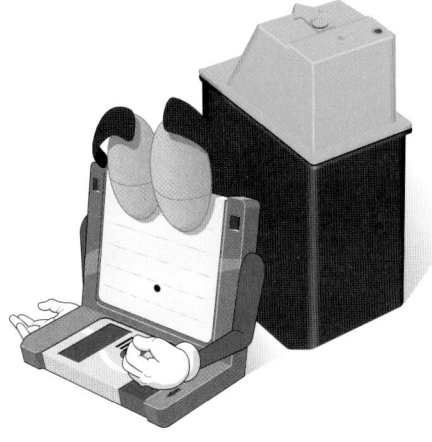

Paper

Ink jet printers accept 8 1/2 by 11-inch paper. Some ink jet printers accept larger paper sizes. Ink jet printers also accept envelopes, labels and transparencies. Make sure you buy items designed specifically for use with ink jet printers.

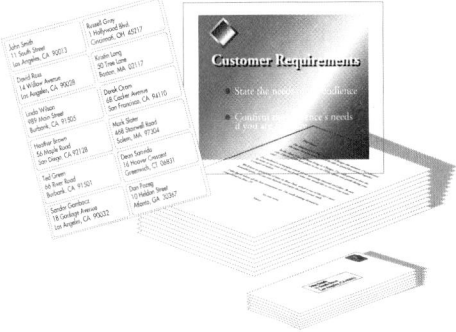

Color

Color ink jet printers are very popular because they are less expensive than color laser printers and still produce high-quality color images.

A color ink jet printer sprays cyan, magenta, yellow and black ink to create images on a page. Lower-cost color ink jet printers create black by mixing the cyan, magenta and yellow ink. The best color images come from printers that offer black as a separate color.

LASER PRINTER

A laser printer is a high-speed printer that is ideal for business and personal documents and for proofing professional graphics work.

A laser printer works like a photocopier to produce high-quality images on a page.

Speed

Most laser printers produce images at a speed of 4 to 20 pages per minute (ppm).

Resolution

The resolution, or quality, of the images produced by a laser printer ranges from 300 to 1200 dots per inch (dpi).

300 dpi   1200 dpi

Ink

Like photocopiers, laser printers use a fine powdered ink, called toner, which comes in a cartridge. When the toner runs out, you buy a new cartridge.

Paper

All laser printers can print on 8 1/2 by 11-inch paper, envelopes, labels and transparencies. Make sure you buy items designed specifically for use with laser printers.

Color

You can buy laser printers that produce color images. A color laser printer is more expensive than a color ink jet printer, but it produces superior output.

Multifunction

A multifunction laser printer can perform more than one task. This type of printer is often able to work as a fax machine, scanner and photocopier as well as a printer.

LASER PRINTER (CONTINUED)

Memory

Laser printers store pages in built-in memory before printing. A typical laser printer comes with 1 MB to 4 MB of memory.

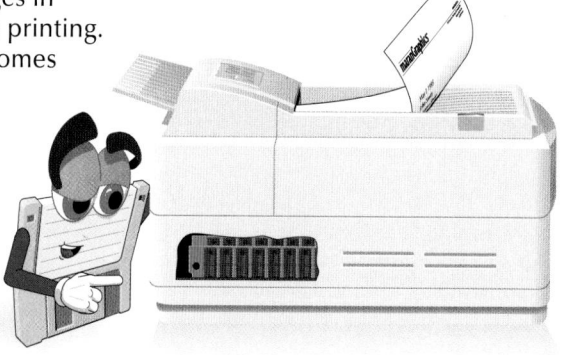

Memory is important for laser printers that produce images at high resolutions, such as 600 dpi. Memory is also important for laser printers that print on larger paper sizes and process complex print jobs.

Laser Printer Languages

A printer language is software that tells a printer how to print a document. There are two types of laser printer languages—PCL and PostScript.

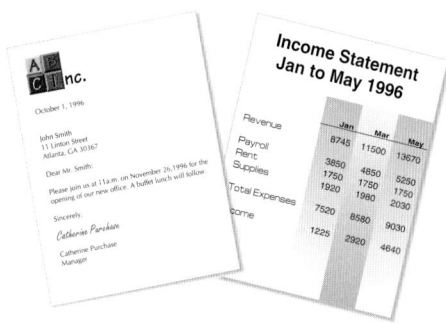

PCL

Most laser printers come with Printer Control Language (PCL). A PCL laser printer is less expensive, but does not offer the graphic capabilities of a PostScript printer. The PCL language is popular for routine office tasks.

PostScript

A PostScript laser printer can handle more complex documents that include various colors, graphics and fonts. The PostScript language is popular in the graphic arts industry.

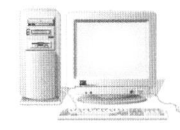

OTHER TYPES OF PRINTERS

There are three other types of printers that let you produce high-quality color images.

Solid Ink Printer

A solid ink printer produces high-quality color images at a relatively low price. This type of printer is ideal for producing crisp color images on regular paper and transparencies.

Thermal-Wax Printer

A thermal-wax printer produces sharp, rich, non-smearing images.

Dye Sublimation Printer

A dye sublimation printer is the most expensive type of printer and produces images that look like color photographs. Dye sublimation printers are also called thermal dye transfer printers.

FONT

A font is a set of characters with a particular design and size. You can use different fonts to make documents more attractive and interesting.

Most printers come with a few built-in fonts, called resident fonts. Resident fonts print faster than the fonts stored on your computer.

TrueType Font

A TrueType font generates characters using mathematical formulas. You can change the size of a TrueType font without distorting the font. A TrueType font will print exactly as it appears on the screen.

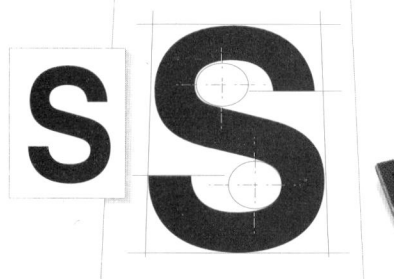

Bitmapped Font

A bitmapped font stores each character as a picture made up of a pattern of dots. If you change the size of a bitmapped font, the font may become distorted.

PRINT BUFFER AND SPOOLER

A computer can send data faster than a printer can accept and process the data. A print spooler or print buffer acts like a dam, holding the data and then releasing it at a speed the printer can handle.

Print Buffer

A print buffer is a section of memory in a printer that stores information you selected to print. When the buffer is full, the computer must wait before sending more data to the printer.

Print Spooler

A print spooler is a program on your computer that stores information you selected to print.

A print spooler can store more information than a print buffer and lets you continue using your computer without having to wait for a document to finish printing. Windows comes with a built-in print spooler.

MONITOR AND VIDEO CARD

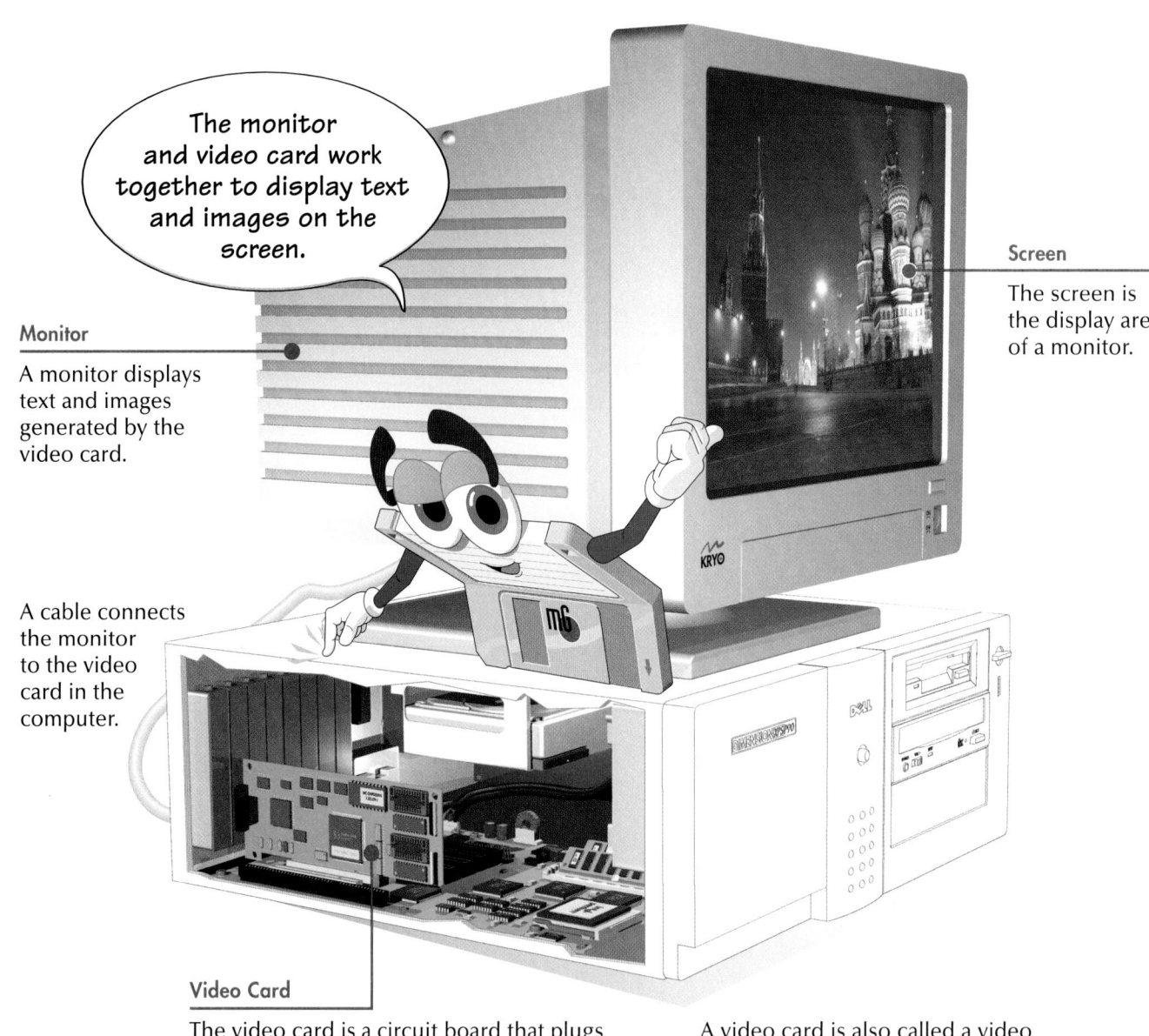

The monitor and video card work together to display text and images on the screen.

Monitor

A monitor displays text and images generated by the video card.

A cable connects the monitor to the video card in the computer.

Screen

The screen is the display area of a monitor.

Video Card

The video card is a circuit board that plugs into an expansion slot inside the computer. The video card translates instructions from the computer to a form the monitor can understand.

A video card is also called a video adapter, video board, graphics adapter, graphics board or graphics card.

CHOOSE A MONITOR

Size

The size of a monitor is measured diagonally across the screen. Common monitor sizes are 14, 15, 17 and 21 inches. Larger monitors are more expensive and are ideal for desktop publishing and working with graphics or large spreadsheets.

Manufacturers usually advertise the diagonal measurement of the picture tube inside the monitor, which is greater than the actual viewing area. Make sure you ask for the size of the viewing area.

Dot Pitch

The dot pitch is the distance between tiny dots on a screen. The dot pitch determines the sharpness of images on the screen. The smaller the dot pitch, the crisper the images. Select a monitor with a dot pitch of 0.28 mm or less.

Non-Interlaced

A non-interlaced monitor greatly reduces screen flicker. These monitors are more expensive than old, interlaced monitors, but help reduce eye strain.

INTERLACED

CHOOSE A MONITOR (CONTINUED)

Refresh Rate

The refresh rate determines the speed that a monitor redraws, or updates, images. The higher the refresh rate, the less flicker on the screen. This helps reduce eye strain.

The refresh rate is measured in hertz (Hz) and tells you the number of times per second the monitor redraws the entire screen. A monitor with a refresh rate of 72 Hz or more is recommended.

Controls

Monitors have controls to adjust the brightness, contrast and other features of the images displayed on the screen. You can find controls on the screen or on the monitor.

Tilt-and-Swivel Base

A tilt-and-swivel base lets you adjust the angle of the screen. This lets you reduce the glare from overhead lighting and view the screen more comfortably.

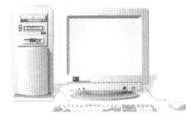

Electromagnetic Radiation

Any device that uses electricity produces electromagnetic radiation (EMR). You can protect yourself from potentially harmful effects by remaining a safe distance away from electrical devices.

Monitors emit EMR, but you can minimize the risk by buying a monitor that meets MPR II guidelines. The MPR II guidelines define acceptable levels of EMR.

You can further minimize the risk by turning off the monitor when it is not in use. Also avoid sitting near the sides or back of a monitor, which emit more EMR than the front.

ENERGY STAR

The Environmental Protection Agency (EPA) developed an energy-saving guideline called ENERGY STAR to reduce wasted energy and the pollution it causes.

When you do not use an ENERGY STAR computer for a period of time, the monitor and computer enter an energy-saving sleep mode. You awaken the computer by moving the mouse or pressing a key on the keyboard.

MONITOR TIPS

Screen Saver

A screen saver is a moving picture or pattern that appears on the screen when you do not use a computer for a period of time.

Screen savers were originally designed to prevent screen burn, which occurs when an image appears in a fixed position for a period of time.

Today's monitors are designed to prevent screen burn, but people still use screen savers for entertainment.

Windows provides several screen savers. You can purchase more sophisticated screen savers at most computer stores.

Glare Filter

A glare filter fits over the front of a monitor to reduce the amount of light reflected off the computer screen. This helps reduce eye strain.

Most glare filters also help block the radiation coming from the front of the monitor.

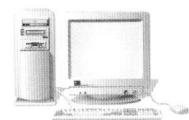

VIDEO CARD MEMORY

A video card has memory chips. These chips temporarily store information before sending it to the monitor.

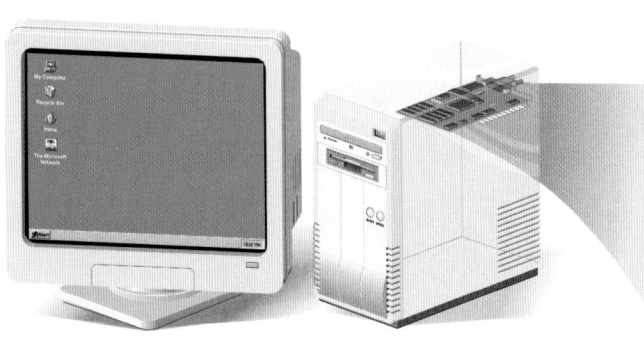

Most computers require at least 1 MB of video card memory.

DRAM

Dynamic Random Access Memory (DRAM) is the least expensive type of memory used on low to mid-range video cards. DRAM is adequate for routine office tasks.

VRAM

Video Random Access Memory (VRAM) is a form of DRAM specifically designed for video cards. VRAM is faster and more expensive than DRAM and is ideal for displaying colorful graphics.

Extended Data Out DRAM (EDO DRAM) and Window RAM (WRAM) are two other types of video card memory.

RESOLUTION

Resolution is measured by the number of horizontal and vertical pixels. A pixel is the smallest element on the screen. Pixel is short for picture element.

> Resolution determines the amount of information a monitor can display.

A multisync monitor lets you adjust the resolution to suit your needs. Other monitors can only display one resolution.

640 x 480	800 x 600	1,024 x 768	1,280 x 1,024
	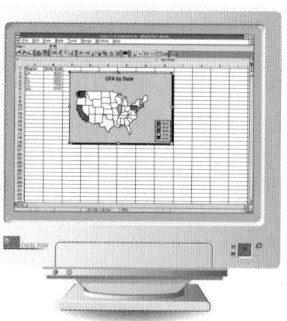	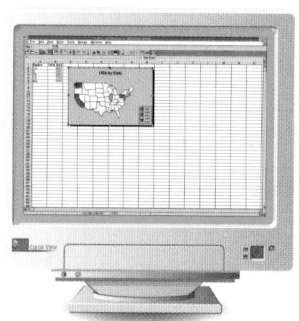	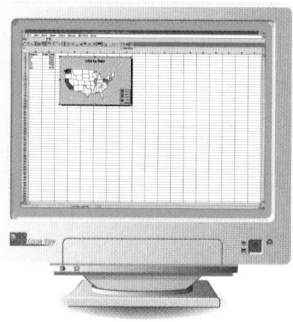

Lower resolutions display larger images so you can see information more clearly.

Higher resolutions display smaller images so you can display more information at once.

COLOR DEPTH

VGA

Video Graphics Array (VGA) monitors display 16 colors at a resolution of 640 x 480. This is the minimum standard for computer systems.

SVGA

Super Video Graphics Array (SVGA) monitors display more colors and higher resolutions than VGA monitors. Most new computer systems offer SVGA.

The number of colors a monitor can display determines how realistic images appear on a screen. More colors result in more realistic images.

16 Colors (4-bit color)

Choppy-looking images.

256 Colors (8-bit color)

Ideal for most home, business and game applications.

65,536 Colors (16-bit color)

Ideal for video and desktop publishing applications. Unless you are a trained professional, it is difficult to distinguish between 16-bit and 24-bit color.

16,777,216 Colors (24-bit color)

Ideal for photographic work. This setting is also called true color because it displays more colors than the human eye can distinguish.

MODEM

A modem lets computers exchange information through telephone lines.

A modem translates computer information into a form that can transmit over phone lines.

Phone Line

You do not need a separate phone line to use a modem. You can use the same phone line for telephone and modem calls. If your telephone and modem share the same line, make sure you turn off the call waiting feature when using your modem, since this feature could disrupt the modem connection.

The receiving modem translates the information it receives into a form the computer can understand.

MODEM APPLICATIONS

Connect to the Internet

A modem lets you connect to the Internet and online services such as America Online and CompuServe. This lets you access a vast amount of information and meet thousands of people with similar interests.

Exchange Information

When traveling or at home, you can use a modem to access information stored on the network at work. You can send and receive electronic messages (e-mail) and work with office files.

Send and Receive Faxes

Most modems can send and receive faxes. With a fax modem, you can create a document on your computer and then fax the document to another computer or fax machine.

When a computer receives a fax, the document appears on the screen. You can review and print the document, but you cannot edit the document unless you have Optical Character Recognition (OCR) software.

TYPES OF MODEMS

Internal Modem

An internal modem is a circuit board that plugs into an expansion slot in a computer. This type of modem is generally less expensive than an external modem, but is more difficult to set up.

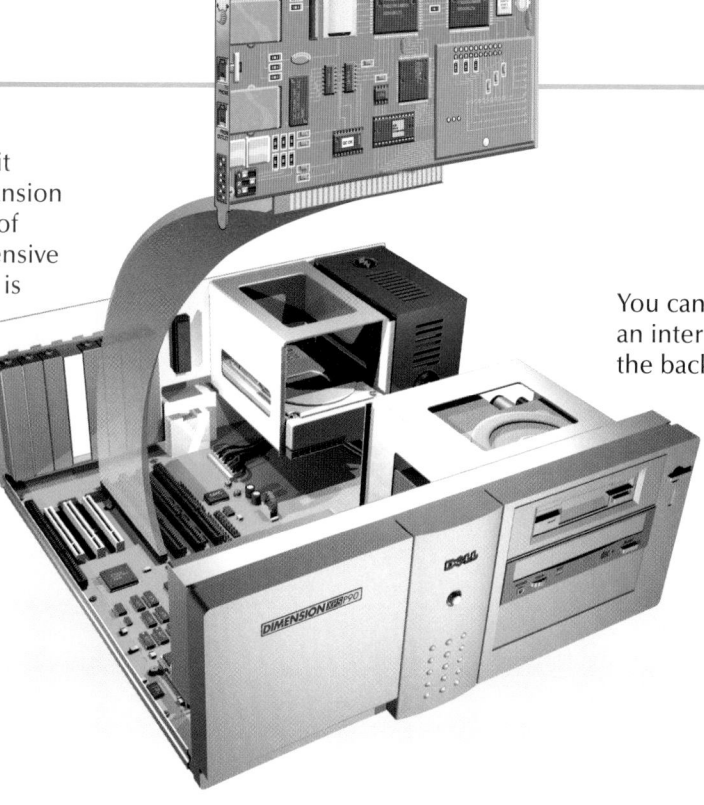

You can see the edge of an internal modem at the back of a computer.

External Modem

An external modem is a small box that plugs into the back of a computer. An external modem takes up room on your desk, but you can use this type of modem with more than one computer.

Status lights on the modem tell you about the current transmission. For example, the RD light is on when the modem is receiving data.

If you are using an external modem with an older computer, make sure the computer uses a 16550 UART chip. This will ensure that the computer can handle current modem speeds. A UART chip controls the flow of information to and from the modem.

MODEM SPEED

The speed of a modem determines how fast it can send and receive information through telephone lines.

Modem speed is measured in bits per second (bps). You should buy a modem with a speed of at least 14,400 bps, but a 28,800 bps modem is recommended.

Modem speeds of 31,200 and 33,600 bps are now available.

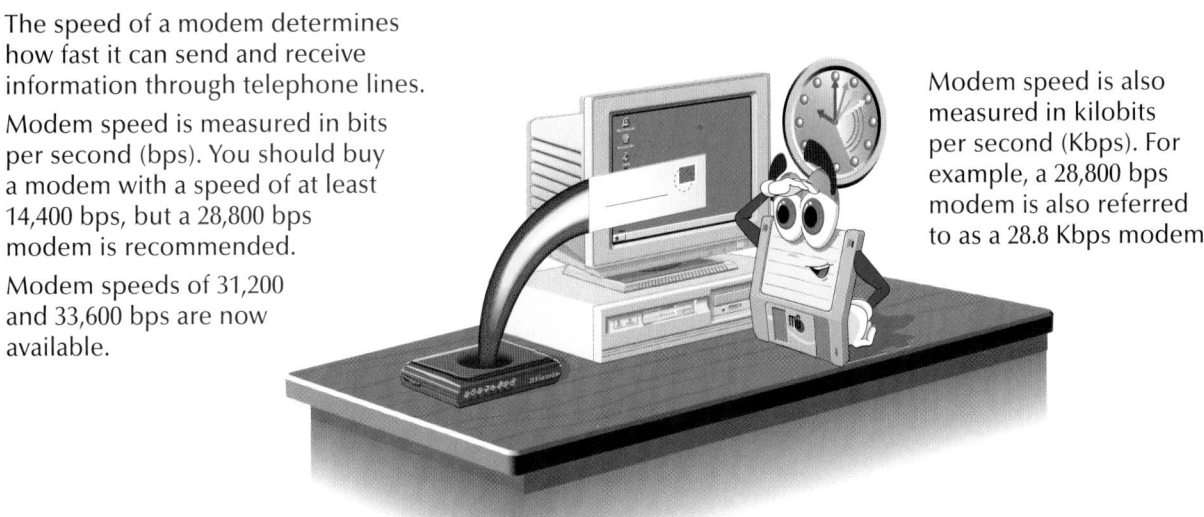

Modem speed is also measured in kilobits per second (Kbps). For example, a 28,800 bps modem is also referred to as a 28.8 Kbps modem.

Save Time and Money

Buy the fastest modem you can afford. Faster modems transfer information more quickly. This will save you time and reduce online service charges and long distance charges.

Line Quality

The speed that information transfers depends on the quality of the phone line. For example, a modem with a speed of 28,800 bps may not reach that speed if the phone line quality is poor.

HOW MODEMS COMMUNICATE

Communications Program

A modem needs a communications program to manage the transmission of information with another modem. This type of program usually comes packaged with a modem.

Handshake

Before exchanging information, modems perform a handshake just as two people shake hands to greet each other. A handshake establishes how the modems will exchange information.

Modems must use the same speed when exchanging information. A fast modem can talk to a slower modem, but they will communicate at the slower speed. You may find that some online services use lower speed modems.

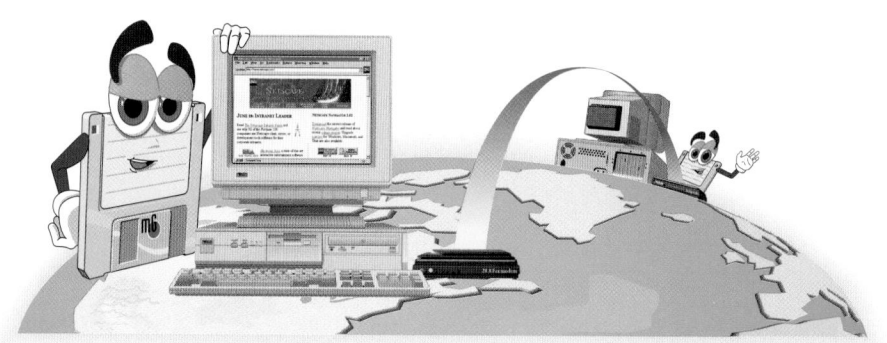

Online

You are online when your modem has successfully connected to another modem. This means the modems are ready and able to exchange information. When your modem is not connected to another modem, you are offline.

DATA COMPRESSION

A modem can compress, or squeeze together, data sent to another modem to speed the transfer of data. How much faster the data transfers depends on the type of file being sent. For example, a text file will compress significantly more than a graphics file.

When the information reaches its intended destination, the receiving modem decompresses the information.

A modem uses error control to ensure that information reliably reaches its destination.

ISDN

Instead of using a modem and a regular phone line, some people use an Integrated Services Digital Network (ISDN) line. ISDN is currently the best choice for a high-speed connection to the Internet.

ISDN transfers information between the Internet Service Provider (ISP) and your home about four times faster than a modem.

ISDN is often used by people working at home who want fast access to information at the office.

SOUND CARD

A sound card lets a computer play and record high-quality sound.

A sound card is a circuit board that plugs into an expansion slot in the computer.

A sound card is also called a sound board or audio card.

Speakers

You need speakers to hear the sound generated by a sound card. Buy speakers with a built-in amplifier between 10 and 30 watts. This will strengthen the sound signal and improve the performance.

SOUND CARD APPLICATIONS

Games and Multimedia Presentations

A sound card lets you hear music, speech and sound effects during games and multimedia presentations.

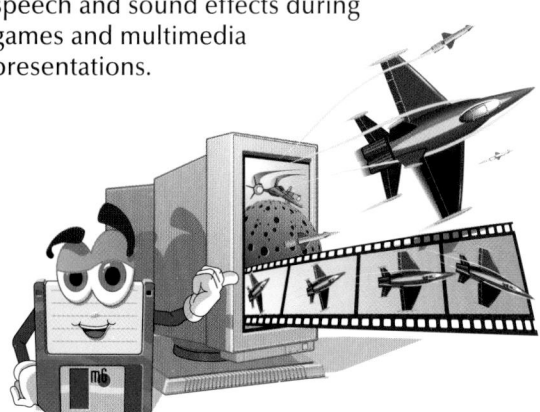

Record Sounds

You can use a sound card to record music, speech and sound effects. You can then add the sounds to documents and presentations. You can also use a sound card to compose music on your computer.

SOUND CARD CONNECTIONS

You can see the edge of a sound card at the back of a computer. A sound card has a port and several jacks where you can plug in external devices.

The edge of your sound card may look different from the sound card shown here.

Joystick

This port lets you connect a joystick or a MIDI device such as a music keyboard.

Line In

This jack lets you connect a cassette or CD player to play music.

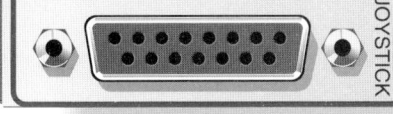

Spk Out

This jack lets you connect speakers or headphones to hear sound generated by a sound card.

Line Out

This jack lets you connect an amplifier to play sound through your home stereo.

Mic In

This jack lets you connect a microphone to record speech and other sounds.

CHOOSE A SOUND CARD

Sampling Size and Rate

The sampling size and rate of a sound card determines the quality of the sound produced.

For good sound quality, buy a sound card with a 16-bit sampling size and a 44.1 KHz sampling rate.

If possible, listen to the sounds produced by various sound cards before making your purchase.

Sound Blaster

Make sure you buy a Sound Blaster compatible sound card to ensure your computer has full sound capabilities.

Full-Duplex

A full-duplex sound card lets you talk and listen at the same time. When using a computer to have a conversation over the Internet, a full-duplex sound card lets people talk at the same time. With a half-duplex card, people must take turns talking.

MIDI

Musical Instrument Digital Interface (MIDI) is a set of instructions that allow computers and musical devices to exchange data. This lets you use a computer to play, record and edit music. Many musicians use MIDI to compose music on a computer.

A sound card that supports MIDI ensures that a computer can generate the sounds often found in games, CD-ROM titles and presentation packages.

There are two ways a sound card can produce MIDI sound.

FM Synthesis

FM synthesis imitates the sounds of musical instruments and speech. This results in less realistic sound. FM synthesis is found on low to mid-range sound cards.

Wavetable Synthesis

Wavetable synthesis uses actual recordings of musical instruments and speech. This results in rich, realistic sound. Wavetable synthesis is found on high-quality sound cards.

SCANNER

A scanner is a device that reads graphics and text into a computer.

Scan Graphics

You can scan graphics such as photographs, drawings and logos into a computer. You can then use the graphics in documents, such as reports or newsletters.

Most scanners come with image editing software, which lets you change the appearance of a scanned graphic.

Scan Text

You can scan text to quickly enter documents into a computer. This lets you scan interesting paper documents and e-mail them to friends or colleagues. You can also scan office documents to store them on your computer for quick access.

Most scanners come with Optical Character Recognition (OCR) software. This software places scanned text into a document that can be edited in a word processor.

TYPES OF SCANNERS

Hand-Held Scanner

A hand-held scanner is the least expensive type of scanner. A hand-held scanner has a scanning width of approximately four inches and is ideal for copying small images, such as signatures, logos and small photographs.

Sheet-Fed Scanner

A sheet-fed scanner produces more reliable scans than a hand-held scanner and is less expensive and more compact than a flatbed scanner. A sheet-fed scanner can only scan single sheets of paper. If you want to scan a page from a book, you have to tear out the page.

Flatbed Scanner

A flatbed scanner is the most expensive and most versatile type of scanner. A flatbed scanner is ideal when you want to scan pages from a book without tearing out the pages.

COLOR

Grayscale Scanner

A grayscale scanner reads images using black, white and shades of gray. A grayscale scanner is ideal for scanning text or when you plan to print scanned images on a black-and-white printer.

Color Scanner

A color scanner is more expensive than a grayscale scanner and reads images using shades of red, blue and green. A color scanner is ideal for scanning images you plan to display in color, such as photographs and illustrations.

Choose the Scanning Mode

When scanning an image, you can choose the scanning mode.

Line Art
The line art mode scans an image using black and white.

Grayscale
The grayscale mode scans an image using black, white and shades of gray.

Color
The color mode scans an image using shades of red, blue and green.

RESOLUTION

The resolution of a scanner determines the amount of detail the scanner can detect.

Scanner resolution is measured in dots per inch (dpi). Some scanners can detect up to 1200 dpi.

Choose the Resolution

Scanning an image at a high resolution results in a clearer, more detailed image, but requires more scanning time and storage space.

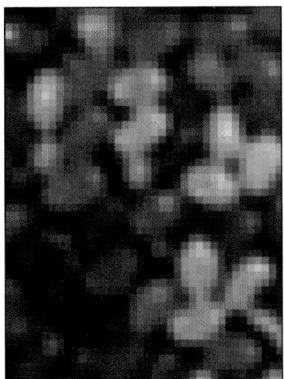

20 dpi

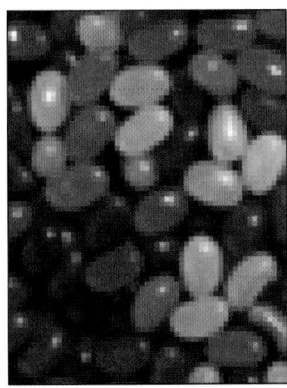

72 dpi

300 dpi

You usually do not need to scan an image at a higher resolution than a printer can produce or a monitor can display.

If you plan to print an image on a 300 dpi printer, you do not need to scan at a resolution higher than 300 dpi. Monitors have a maximum resolution of 72 dpi. If you plan to display an image on a monitor, you do not need to scan at a resolution higher than 72 dpi.

PROCESSING

MEMORY

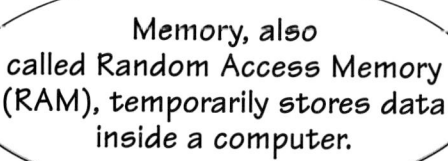

Memory, also called Random Access Memory (RAM), temporarily stores data inside a computer.

Memory works like a blackboard that is constantly overwritten with new data. The data stored in memory disappears when you turn off the computer.

MEMORY SIZE

The amount of memory determines the number of programs a computer can run at once and how fast programs will operate.

Memory is measured in bytes. You should buy a computer with at least 8 MB of memory, but 16 MB is recommended.

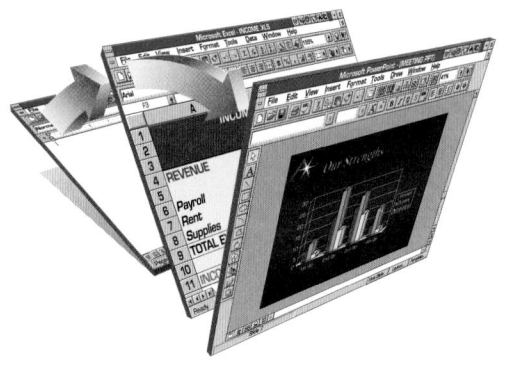

You can improve the performance of a computer by adding more memory.

PROGRAM REQUIREMENTS

A program will usually tell you the minimum amount of memory your computer needs to use the program.

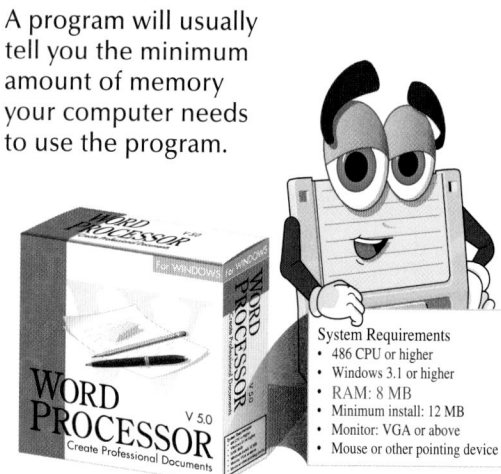

System Requirements
- 486 CPU or higher
- Windows 3.1 or higher
- RAM: 8 MB
- Minimum install: 12 MB
- Monitor: VGA or above
- Mouse or other pointing device

DRAM

Dynamic RAM (DRAM) is a type of memory chip that makes up the main memory in many computer systems.

Extended Data Out DRAM (EDO DRAM) is a faster type of memory chip found in most computer systems.

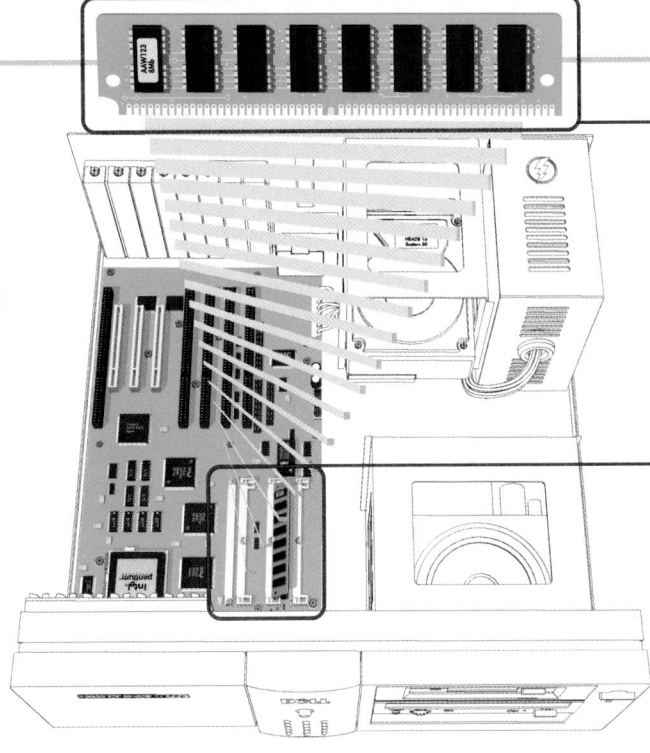

SIMM

A Single In-line Memory Module (SIMM) is a circuit board that holds memory chips. You can add more memory to a computer by inserting additional SIMMs.

SIMM Socket

A SIMM socket is a socket on the motherboard where you plug in a SIMM.

VIRTUAL MEMORY

If you have limited memory or you have many programs open, your computer may need to use part of the hard drive to simulate more memory.

This simulated memory is called virtual memory and allows the computer to continue operating, but at a much slower speed.

ROM

Unlike RAM, Read-Only Memory (ROM) is permanent and cannot be changed. ROM stores instructions that help prepare the computer for use each time you turn on the computer.

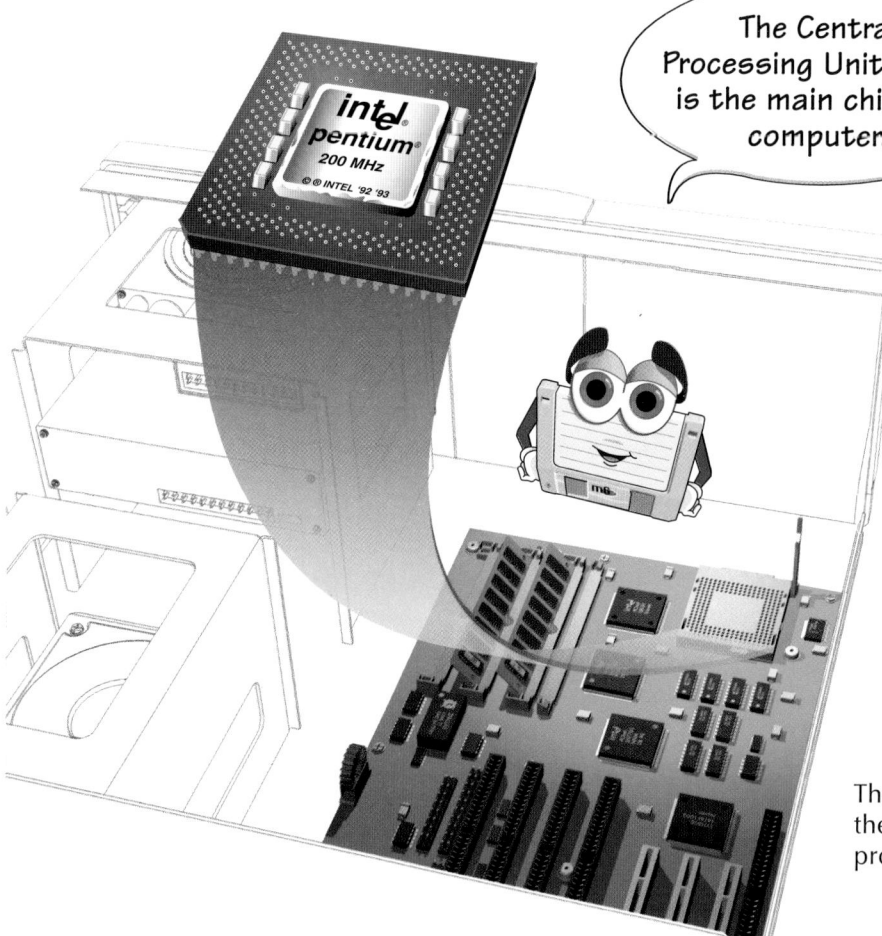

The Central Processing Unit (CPU) is the main chip in a computer.

The CPU processes instructions, performs calculations and manages the flow of information through a computer system. The CPU performs millions of calculations every second.

The CPU is also called the microprocessor or processor.

CPU COMPLEXITY

Imagine a U.S. road map printed on a fingernail and you can imagine the complexity of a CPU. The elements in a CPU can be as small as 0.35 microns wide. By comparison, a human hair is about 100 microns wide.

The manufacturing plants that produce CPUs are tens of thousands of times cleaner than hospital operating rooms. Ultra-sensitive dust filtering systems are needed to eliminate particles that could damage the CPUs.

CHOOSE A CPU

There are several factors that determine the performance of a CPU.

Manufacturer

CPUs for personal computers are made by companies such as Intel, AMD, Cyrix and Motorola. Intel chips are the most popular.

Generation

Each new generation of CPUs is more powerful than the one before. Newer CPUs can process more instructions at a time.

CPU generations include the 486, Pentium (586) and Pentium Pro (686). The older 386 generation is obsolete.

Speed

Each CPU generation is available in several speeds. The CPU speed is a major factor in determining how fast a computer operates. The faster the speed, the faster the computer operates.

The speed of a CPU is measured in megahertz (MHz), or millions of cycles per second.

486

Older computers use the 486 chip. There are four types of 486 chips.

486SX	Does not include a math coprocessor.
486DX	Includes a math coprocessor to speed the performance of complex math calculations.
486DX2	Performs twice as fast as the 486DX.
486DX4	Performs three times as fast as the 486DX.

Pentium

The Pentium chip is ideal for computers using Windows 3.1 and Windows 95. Pentium chips are available with speeds of 75, 100, 133, 166 and 200 MHz.

When buying a new computer, do not consider anything less than a Pentium chip.

Pentium Pro

The Pentium Pro chip is ideal for computers that use powerful operating systems such as Windows NT and Unix.

Pentium Pro chips are available with speeds of 150, 166, 180 and 200 MHz.

Intel plans to add multimedia extensions (MMX) to the Pentium and Pentium Pro chips. This will dramatically improve the performance of multimedia tasks such as the processing of graphics, video and sound.

You can increase the processing power of a computer by replacing the CPU chip with a new one.

OverDrive Chip
An OverDrive chip lets you improve the performance of your computer without having to buy a new computer.

You cannot upgrade all CPU chips. Even if you can upgrade an old chip, the rest of your computer may not be fast enough to make it worthwhile. In this situation, the best solution is to buy a new computer.

■ A tiny handle secures the CPU on the motherboard.

ZIF Socket

A Zero Insertion Force (ZIF) socket lets you easily remove and then replace the CPU.

MEMORY CACHE

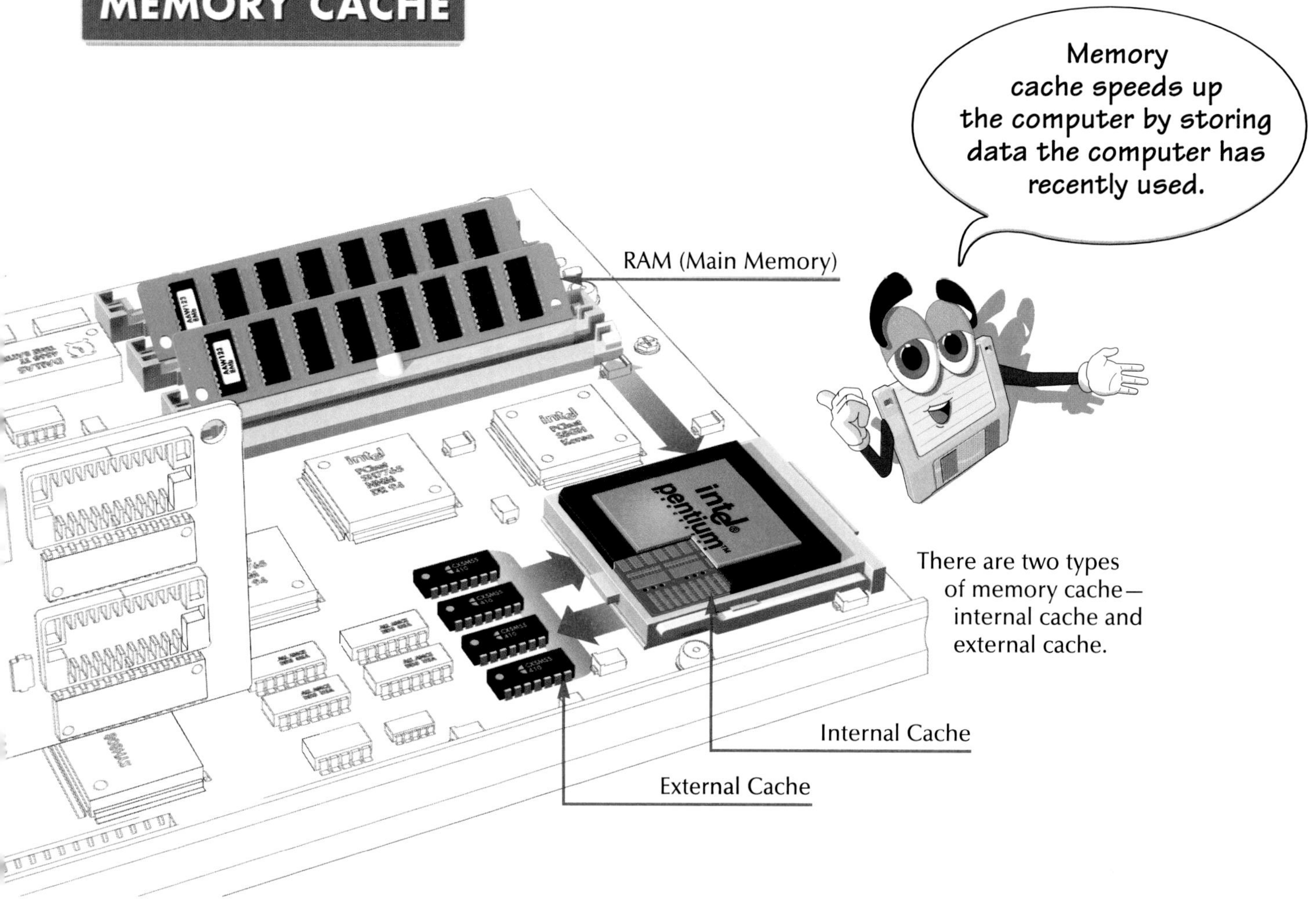

Memory cache speeds up the computer by storing data the computer has recently used.

RAM (Main Memory)

intel pentium

There are two types of memory cache—internal cache and external cache.

Internal Cache

External Cache

INTERNAL CACHE

When the computer needs data, the computer first looks in the internal cache. Internal cache is on the CPU chip and provides the fastest way for the computer to get data. Internal cache is also called L1 or primary cache.

RECENTLY USED DATA

intel pentium

EXTERNAL CACHE

If the computer cannot find the data it needs in the internal cache, the computer looks in the external cache. External cache is on the motherboard and consists of Static RAM (SRAM) chips.

External cache is slower than internal cache, but is much faster than RAM. External cache is also called L2 or secondary cache.

RECENTLY USED DATA

RAM

If the computer cannot find the data it needs in the internal or external cache, the computer must get the data from the slower main memory, called RAM.

Each time the computer requests data from RAM, the computer places a copy of the data in the memory cache. This process constantly updates the memory cache so it always contains the most recently used data.

USING MEMORY CACHE

Using memory cache is similar to working with documents in your office. When you need information, you look for information in a specific order. Each step along the way takes up more of your valuable time.

❶ Look through documents on your desk (internal cache).

❷ Look through documents in your desk drawer (external cache).

❸ Look through documents in your filing cabinet (RAM).

Working without memory cache would be similar to looking through the filing cabinet each time you need a document.

BUS

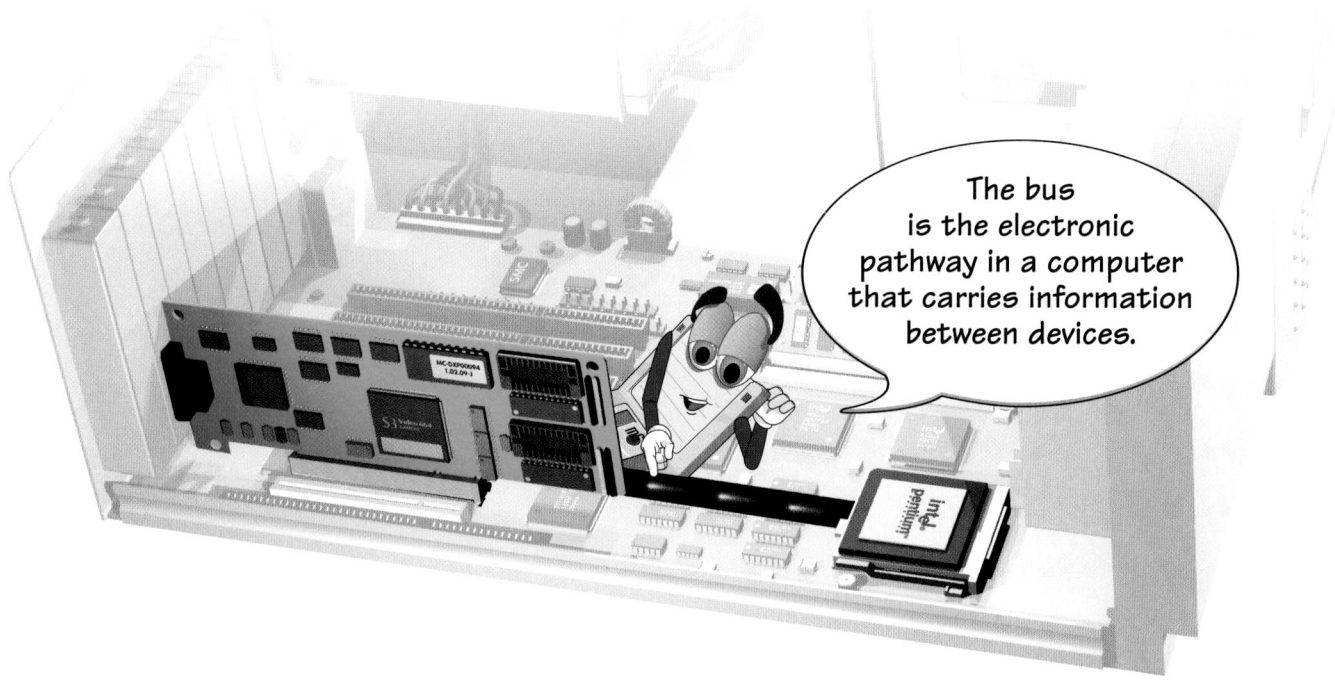

The bus is the electronic pathway in a computer that carries information between devices.

Bus Width

The bus width is similar to the number of lanes on a highway. The greater the width, the more data can flow along the bus at a time. Bus width is measured in bits. Eight bits equals one character.

Bus Speed

The bus speed is similar to the speed limit on a highway. The higher the speed, the faster data travels along the bus. Bus speed is measured in megahertz (MHz), or millions of cycles per second.

TYPES OF BUSES

ISA Bus

The Industry Standard Architecture (ISA) bus is the slowest and oldest type of bus. This bus is ideal for transferring information to and from a slow device, such as a modem. The ISA bus has a width of 16 bits and a speed of 8 MHz.

The ISA bus is found in 486, Pentium and Pentium Pro computers.

VL-Bus

The VESA Local Bus (VL-Bus) transfers information much faster than the ISA bus. This bus is primarily used to send data to a monitor. The VL-Bus has a width of 32 bits and speeds of up to 40 MHz.

The VL-Bus is found in 486 computers.

PCI Bus

The Peripheral Component Interconnect (PCI) bus is the most sophisticated type of bus. This bus can handle many high-speed devices. The PCI bus can have a width of 32 or 64 bits and speeds of up to 66 MHz.

The PCI bus is found in Pentium and Pentium Pro computers.

The PCI bus supports Plug and Play, which lets you add new devices to a computer without complex installation procedures.

STORAGE DEVICES

HARD DRIVE

The hard drive is the primary device that a computer uses to store information.

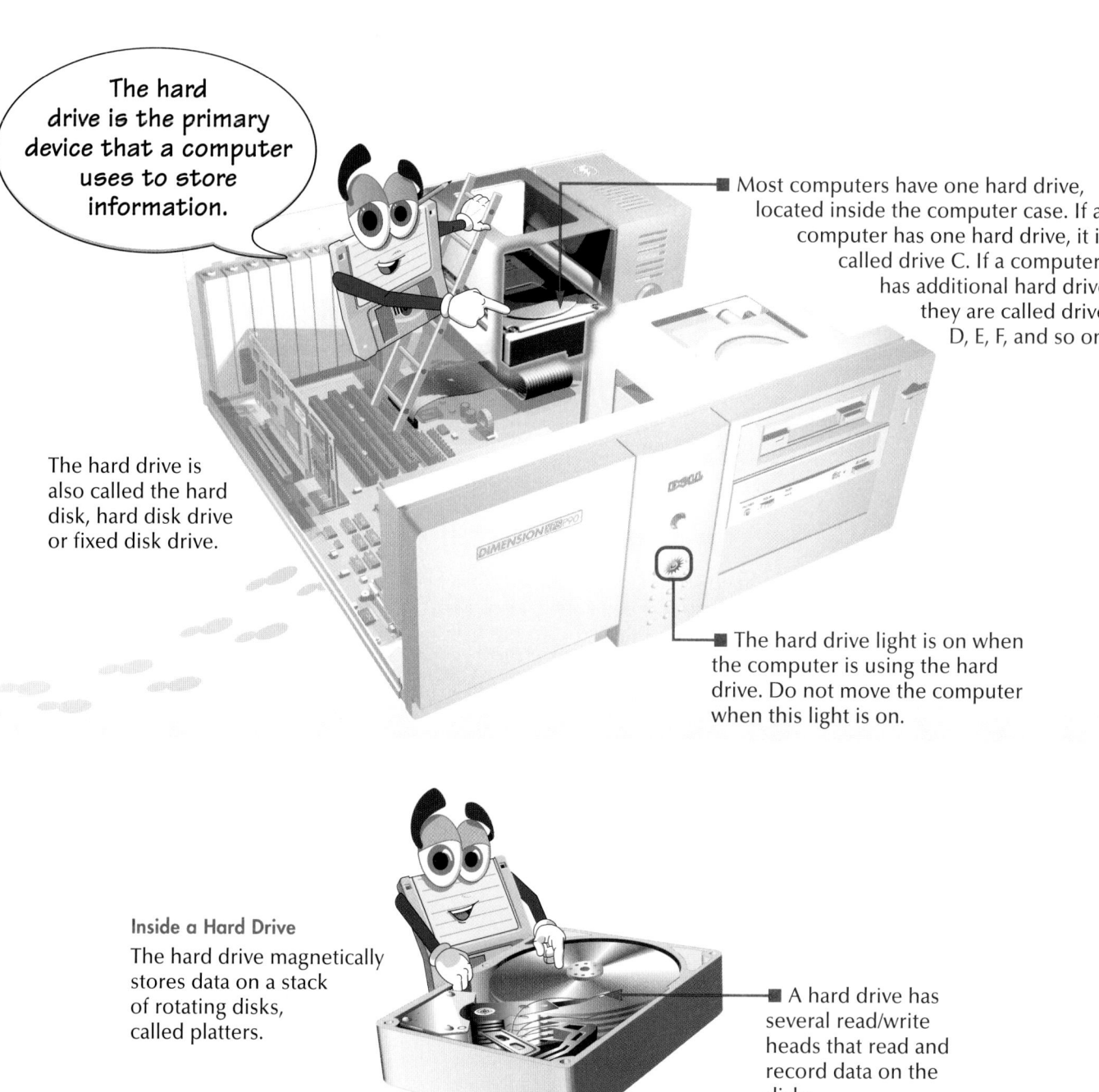

Most computers have one hard drive, located inside the computer case. If a computer has one hard drive, it is called drive C. If a computer has additional hard drives, they are called drives D, E, F, and so on.

The hard drive is also called the hard disk, hard disk drive or fixed disk drive.

The hard drive light is on when the computer is using the hard drive. Do not move the computer when this light is on.

Inside a Hard Drive

The hard drive magnetically stores data on a stack of rotating disks, called platters.

A hard drive has several read/write heads that read and record data on the disks.

HARD DRIVE CONTENTS

Program Files

A hard drive stores your programs. When you buy a new program, you must install, or copy, the program files to your hard drive before you can use the program.

Data Files

A hard drive stores your data files such as documents, spreadsheets and graphics.

Programs come on a CD-ROM disc or several floppy disks.

STORE FILES

Save Files

When you are creating a document, the computer stores the document in temporary memory. If you want to store a document for future use, you must save the document to the hard drive. If you do not save the document, the document will be lost when there is a power failure or you turn off the computer.

Organize Files

Like a filing cabinet, a hard drive uses folders or directories to organize information.

CHOOSE A HARD DRIVE

Capacity

The amount of information a hard drive can store is measured in bytes.

A hard drive with a capacity of 850 MB to 1.2 GB will suit most home and business users.

Purchase the largest hard drive you can afford. New programs and data will quickly fill a hard drive. For example, Microsoft Word is a word processing program that requires about 16 MB of hard drive space. Windows 95 is an operating system that requires about 40 MB.

Average Access Time

The average access time is the speed at which a hard drive finds data.

The average access time is measured in milliseconds (ms). One millisecond equals 1/1000 of a second. Most hard drives have an average access time of 9 to 14 ms. The lower the average access time, the faster the hard drive.

CONNECTION TYPE

IDE

Integrated Drive Electronics (IDE) is the least expensive way to connect a hard drive to a computer.

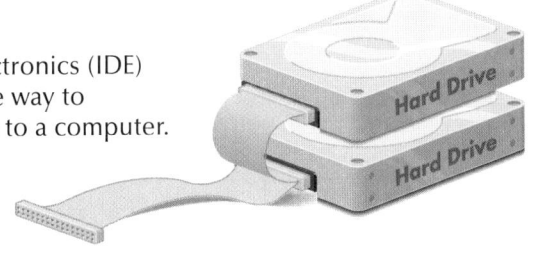

IDE can support two hard drives. Each drive cannot have a storage capacity of more than 528 MB.

EIDE

Most new computers come with Enhanced IDE (EIDE). EIDE is faster and can connect more devices to a computer than IDE.

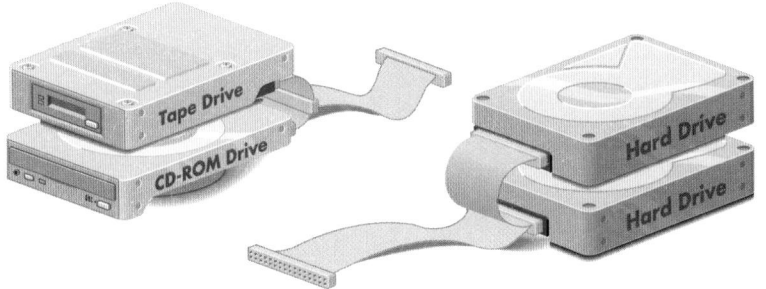

EIDE can support up to four devices. These devices can be hard drives with storage capacities over 528 MB, or other devices such as CD-ROM and tape drives.

SCSI

Small Computer System Interface (SCSI) is the fastest, most flexible, but most expensive way to connect a hard drive and other devices to a computer. SCSI is pronounced "scuzzy."

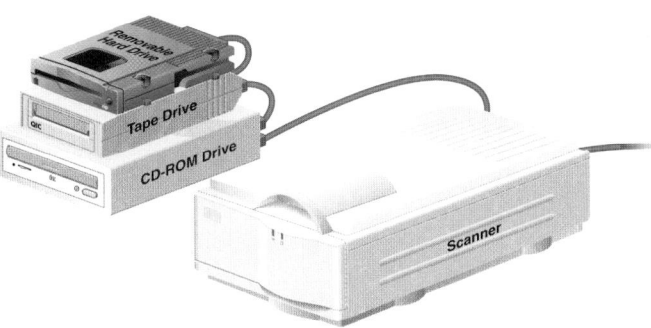

SCSI can connect up to seven devices. These devices can include removable hard drives, CD-ROM drives, tape drives, scanners and printers.

REMOVABLE HARD DRIVE

Removable hard drives are available. Popular removable hard drives include Jaz and Zip drives.

A Jaz drive can store up to 1 GB (1,000 MB) of data, whereas a Zip drive can store 100 MB of data.

Archive Data

You can use a removable hard drive to store old or rarely used files. You can then remove the files from your computer to provide more storage space.

Protect Data

You can use a removable hard drive to store confidential information or backup copies of data. You can then protect the data by placing the disks in a safe place on nights and weekends.

Transfer Data

You can use a removable hard drive to transfer large amounts of information between computers. For example, you can take work home or transfer information to a colleague.

DISK CACHE

The disk cache speeds up the computer by storing data the computer has recently used.

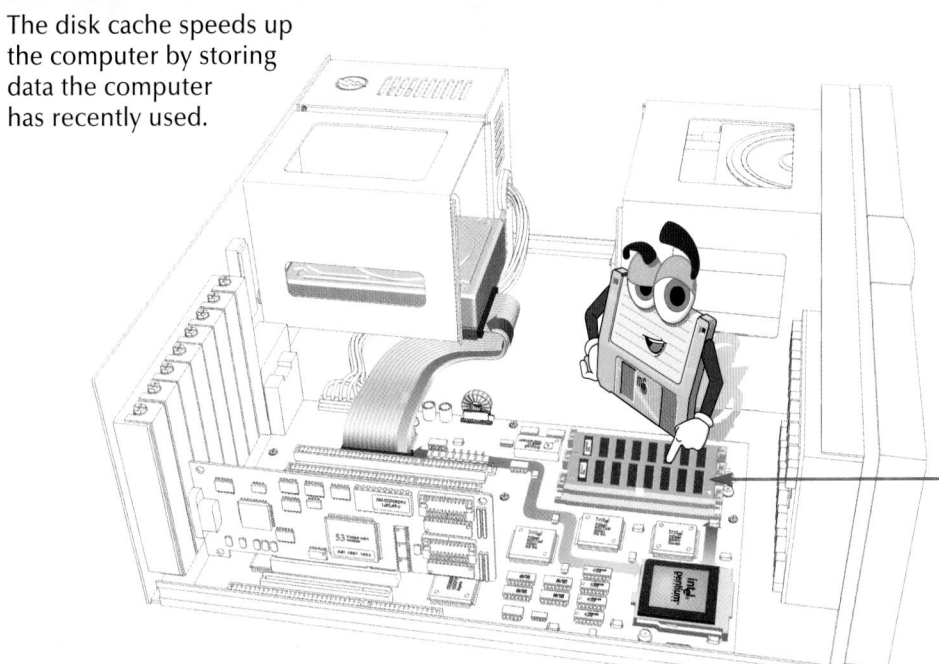

■ The disk cache is an area of memory where the computer stores recently used data.

When the computer needs data, the computer first looks in the disk cache. The disk cache can supply data thousands of times faster than the hard drive.

If the computer cannot find the data it needs in the disk cache, the computer looks on the hard drive.

Each time the computer requests data from the hard drive, the computer places a copy of the data in the disk cache. This process constantly updates the disk cache so it always contains the most recently used data.

OPTIMIZE A HARD DRIVE

Defragment a Drive

A fragmented hard drive stores parts of a file in many different locations. To retrieve a file, the computer must search many areas of the drive.

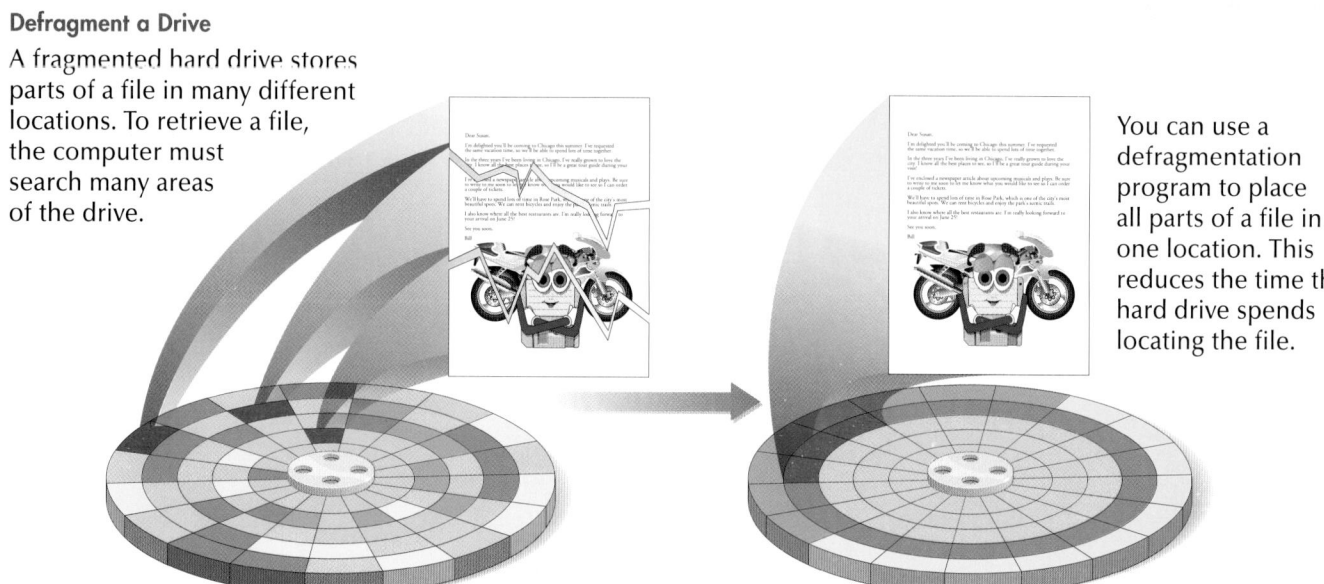

You can use a defragmentation program to place all parts of a file in one location. This reduces the time the hard drive spends locating the file.

Defragmenting your hard drive once a month can improve the performance of the computer.

Windows 95 includes a defragmentation program called Defragmenter.

Repair a Drive

You can improve the performance of a computer by using a disk repair program to search for and repair disk errors. You should check a hard drive for errors at least once a month.

Windows 95 includes a disk repair program called ScanDisk.

CREATE MORE DISK SPACE

Archive Information

Store old or rarely used files on a tape cartridge, removable hard disk or floppy disks. You can then remove the files from your computer to provide more storage space.

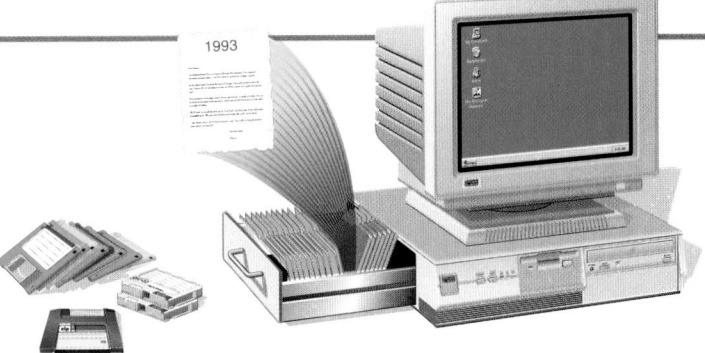

Delete Files

Delete all files and programs you no longer need from your computer. Clean up a hard drive as you would clean up old documents stored in a filing cabinet.

Data Compression

You can compress, or squeeze together, the files stored on a hard drive. This can double the amount of information the drive can store.

You should only compress a hard drive if it is running out of space to store new information and you have tried all other ways of increasing the available storage space.

Windows 95 includes a disk compression program called DriveSpace.

PROTECT A HARD DRIVE

Virus

A virus is a program that disrupts the normal operation of a computer. A virus can cause a variety of problems, such as the appearance of annoying messages on the screen or the destruction of information on the hard drive.

Floppy Disk

If you receive files on a floppy disk from a colleague or friend, make sure you check for viruses before using the files.

Modem

Files you receive through a modem may contain viruses. Make sure you check for viruses before using any files you receive through a modem.

Anti-Virus Programs

You should regularly use an anti-virus program to check for viruses on your computer. You can get anti-virus programs at most computer stores and on the Internet.

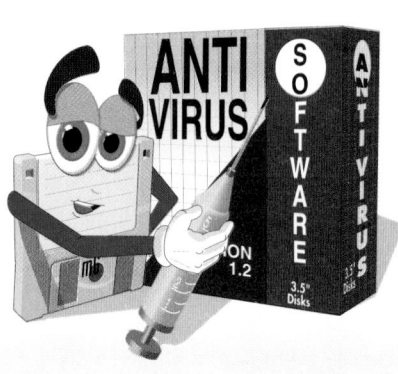

Back Up Data

You should copy the files stored on your hard drive to floppy disks or tape cartridges. This provides extra copies in case the original files are stolen or damaged due to viruses or computer failure.

Windows 95 comes with a backup program called Backup.

Back Up Work

You only need to back up your own work. You do not need to back up programs stored on your computer since you can use the original program disks to re-install the programs. Make sure you keep the program disks in a safe place.

Back Up Frequently

Create and then strictly follow a backup schedule. Hard drive disasters always seem to happen right after you miss a scheduled backup. Most people back up their hard drive once a day or once a week.

FLOPPY DRIVE

A floppy drive stores and retrieves information on floppy disks.

A computer has one or two floppy drives. If a computer has one floppy drive, the drive is called drive A. If a computer has two floppy drives, the second drive is called drive B.

A floppy drive stores information on floppy disks, or diskettes. A floppy disk is a removable device that magnetically stores data.

TYPES OF FLOPPY DISKS

3.5 Inch Floppy Disk

Most floppy drives use 3.5 inch floppy disks. Inside a 3.5 inch floppy disk is a thin, plastic, flexible disk that magnetically records information. The word floppy refers to this flexible disk.

5.25 Inch Floppy Disk

Older computers use 5.25 inch floppy disks.

Install New Programs

Programs you buy at a computer store can come on one or several floppy disks. Before you can use a program, you must install, or copy, the contents of the floppy disks onto your computer.

Transfer Data

You can use floppy disks to transfer data from one computer to another. This lets you give data to friends and colleagues.

Increase Hard Drive Space

You can increase the available space on your computer by copying old or rarely used files to floppy disks. You can then remove the files from the computer to provide more storage space.

Back Up Data

You can protect the files stored on your computer by copying the files to floppy disks. These files will serve as backup copies if your hard drive fails or you accidentally erase important files.

FLOPPY DRIVE continued

INSERT A FLOPPY DISK

Push the floppy disk gently into the drive, label side up. Most drives make a "click" sound when you have fully inserted the disk.

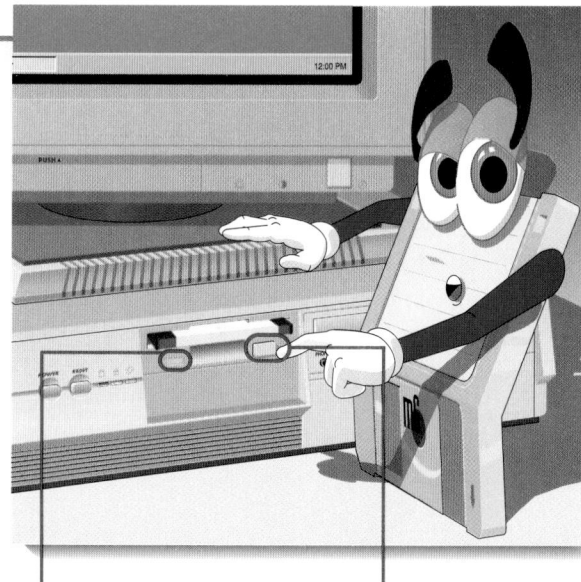

■ This light is on when the computer is using the floppy disk. Do not remove the disk when this light is on.

■ To remove the floppy disk, press this button.

PROTECT A FLOPPY DISK

You can prevent erasing and recording information on a floppy disk by sliding the tab to the write-protected position.

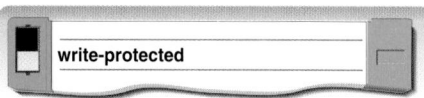

write-protected

You **cannot** erase and record information.

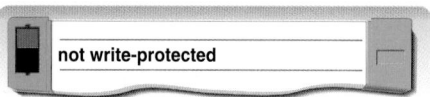

not write-protected

You **can** erase and record information.

Make sure you keep floppy disks away from magnets, which can damage the information stored on the disks. Also make sure you do not store floppy disks in extremely hot or cold locations and try not to spill liquids such as coffee or soda on the disks.

CHOOSE A FLOPPY DISK

Floppy Disk Capacity

Floppy disks come in two storage capacities. High-density disks store more information than double-density disks.

Double-Density

A double-density (DD) floppy disk can store 720 K of information. This disk has only one hole at the top of the disk.

High-Density

A high-density (HD) floppy disk can store 1.44 MB of information. This disk has two holes at the top of the disk and usually displays the letters HD.

Formatted Floppy Disk

A floppy disk must be formatted before you can use it to store data. Formatting a disk prepares the disk for use by dividing it into tracks and sectors. This organizes the disk so the computer can store and retrieve information.

You can save time by purchasing ready-to-use, formatted floppy disks.

Double-Sided Floppy Disk

A double-sided (DS) floppy disk stores data on both sides of the disk. Older, single-sided (SS) disks stored data on only one side of the disk.

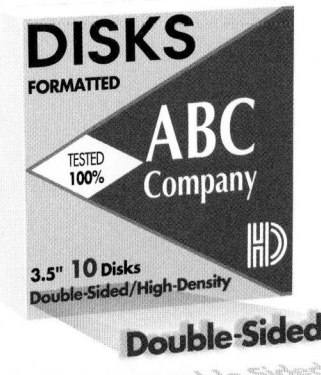

CD-ROM DRIVE

> A CD-ROM drive is a device that reads information stored on compact discs.

Most CD-ROM drives are located inside the computer case. External CD-ROM drives that connect to the computer by a cable are also available.

CD-ROM DISC

A CD-ROM disc is the same type of disc you buy at a music store.

A single CD-ROM disc can store more than 600 MB of data. This is equal to an entire set of encyclopedias or over 400 floppy disks. The large storage capacity of CD-ROM discs leaves more room for storing large images, animation and video.

CD-ROM stands for Compact Disc-Read Only Memory. Read-only means you cannot change the information stored on a disc.

CD-ROM APPLICATIONS

Install Programs

The large storage capacity of a CD-ROM disc makes installing new programs on your computer easy. A program that requires 20 floppy disks can easily fit on a single CD-ROM disc.

Play CD-ROM Titles

There are thousands of educational and entertaining CD-ROM discs available. Most CD-ROM titles are interactive. You can move through topics covered on a disc at your own pace and find topics of interest in seconds.

Play Music CDs

You can play music CDs on a CD-ROM drive while you work.

MULTIMEDIA

A CD-ROM disc can store multimedia presentations.

Multimedia refers to the combination of text, graphics, sound, animation and video. Multimedia provides a powerful way of communicating information.

There are thousands of multimedia titles available to inform and entertain you. You can buy multimedia titles at most computer stores.

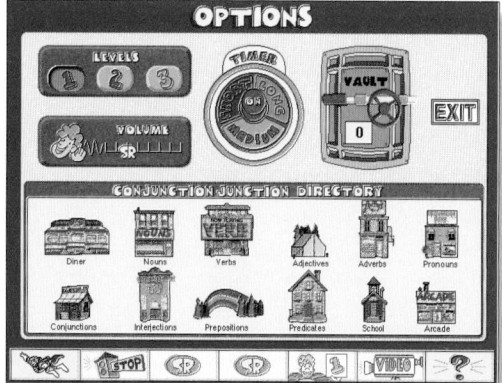

Children

Hundreds of multimedia titles are available to stimulate a child's imagination. There are stories that offer magical adventures and games for children of all ages. Many games teach basic skills such as reading, writing, spelling and math.

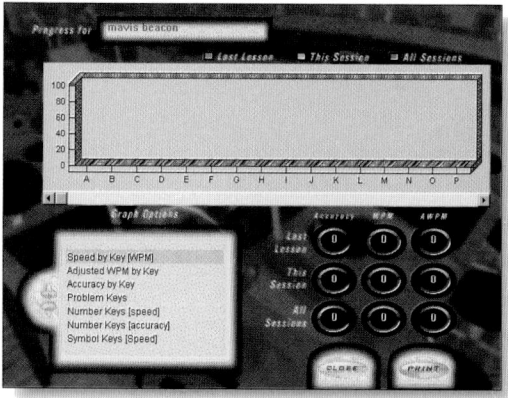

Education

There are many stimulating and comprehensive educational titles that can teach you new skills. You can learn how to type, renovate your home or speak a new language.

Games

Multimedia games can keep you entertained for hours. You can defend your world from invading aliens, play golf or football, try to defeat the dealer in a blackjack game or enjoy the sights and sounds of real flight.

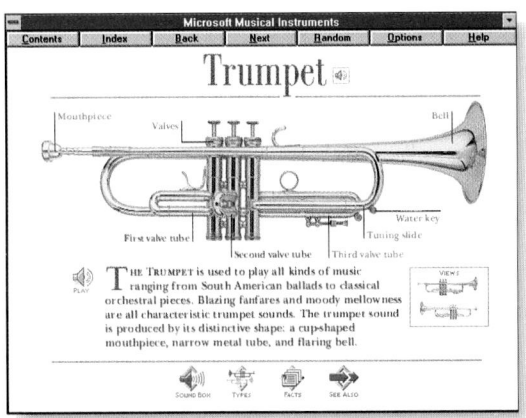

General Interest

You can use multimedia titles to explore the world around you. Learn about the instruments in an orchestra, discover how to treat common illnesses, stroll through an art gallery or take a trip through the solar system.

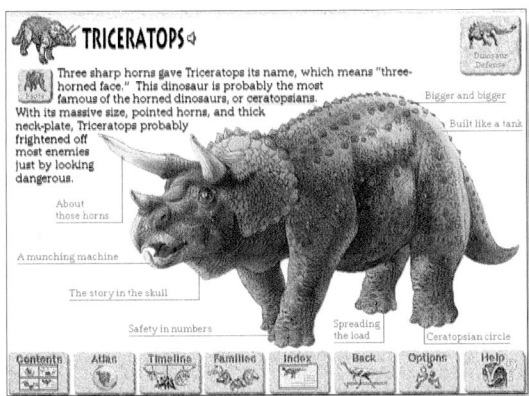

Reference

CD-ROM discs that store large collections of information, such as encyclopedias, maps, magazine articles and dictionaries, are available. You can instantly search for information stored on a disc.

Time-Sensitive Discs

Some CD-ROM discs, such as a disc containing telephone numbers, are time-sensitive and will soon become outdated.

If you need the information to be up-to-date, ask the manufacturer for updated versions of the disc. Some CD-ROM titles, such as Microsoft Encarta, let you access updated information on the Internet.

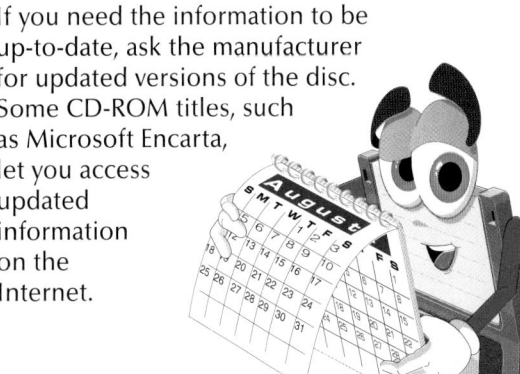

CHOOSE A CD-ROM DRIVE

Speed

The speed of a CD-ROM drive determines how fast a disc spins. With faster speeds, information can transfer from a disc to the computer more quickly, which results in better performance.

The speed of a CD-ROM drive is also called the data transfer rate or throughput.

Speed is very important when viewing video and animation often found in games and encyclopedias. Slow speeds will result in jerky performances.

Single (1x)	150 Kbps
Double (2x)	300 Kbps
Triple (3x)	450 Kbps
Quad (4x)	600 Kbps
Six (6x)	900 Kbps
Eight (8x)	1,200 Kbps

These are the available speeds. You should buy a CD-ROM drive with a speed of at least 600 Kbps.

Average Access Time

The average access time indicates how quickly a CD-ROM drive can find information stored on a disc. Average access times typically range from 150 ms to 300 ms.

The lower the average access time, the quicker you can find what you are looking for on a disc containing large amounts of information.

Multisession

Information can be stored on a disc at several different times, called sessions. For example, with a Photo CD, you can have a photofinisher record slides on a disc and then add more slides to the disc at a later date.

Older, single session CD-ROM drives can only read the original data recorded on a disc. Multisession CD-ROM drives can read both the original data and the data that was later added to the disc.

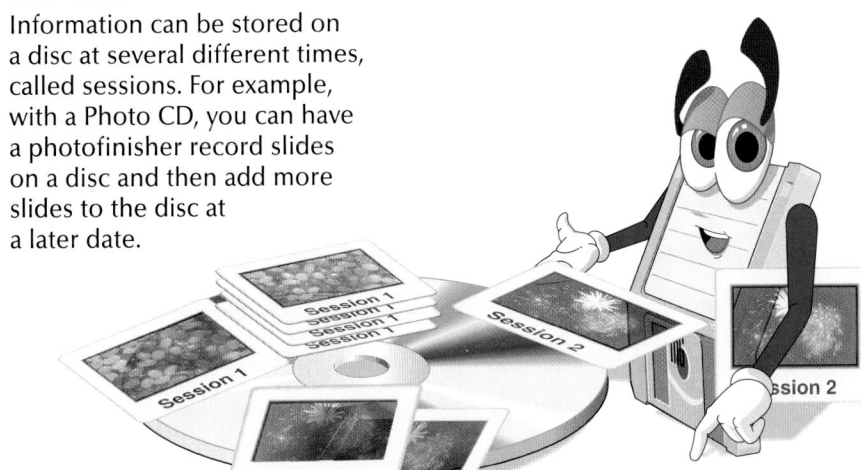

WORK WITH A CD-ROM DISC

Insert a Disc

■ To insert or remove a disc, press this button.

■ A tray slides out. Place the disc, label side up, on the tray. To close the tray, press the button again.

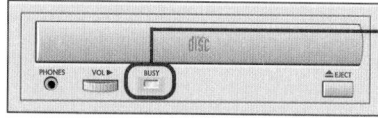

■ This light is on when the CD-ROM drive is accessing information on the disc.

Headphones

You can use headphones to listen to recorded sounds on a disc. Headphones are useful in noisy environments or when you want to listen to a disc privately.

Handle a Disc

When handling a CD-ROM disc, hold the disc around the edges.

Protect a Disc

When you finish using a disc, make sure you place the disc back in its protective case. Do not stack discs on top of each other.

CD-ROM ALTERNATIVES

CD-Recordable

CD-Recordable (CD-R) drives are available if you want to store your own information on a disc. These drives are often used to back up hard drives or to distribute and archive information.

DVD-ROM

The Digital Video Disc-ROM (DVD-ROM) drive is similar to a CD-ROM drive. A DVD-ROM disc has a storage capacity starting at 4.7 GB, which equals over six CD-ROM discs.

A DVD-ROM disc can hold a two hour, full-screen movie with better quality than a VHS tape.

A DVD-ROM drive is able to read your CD-ROM discs.

TAPE DRIVE

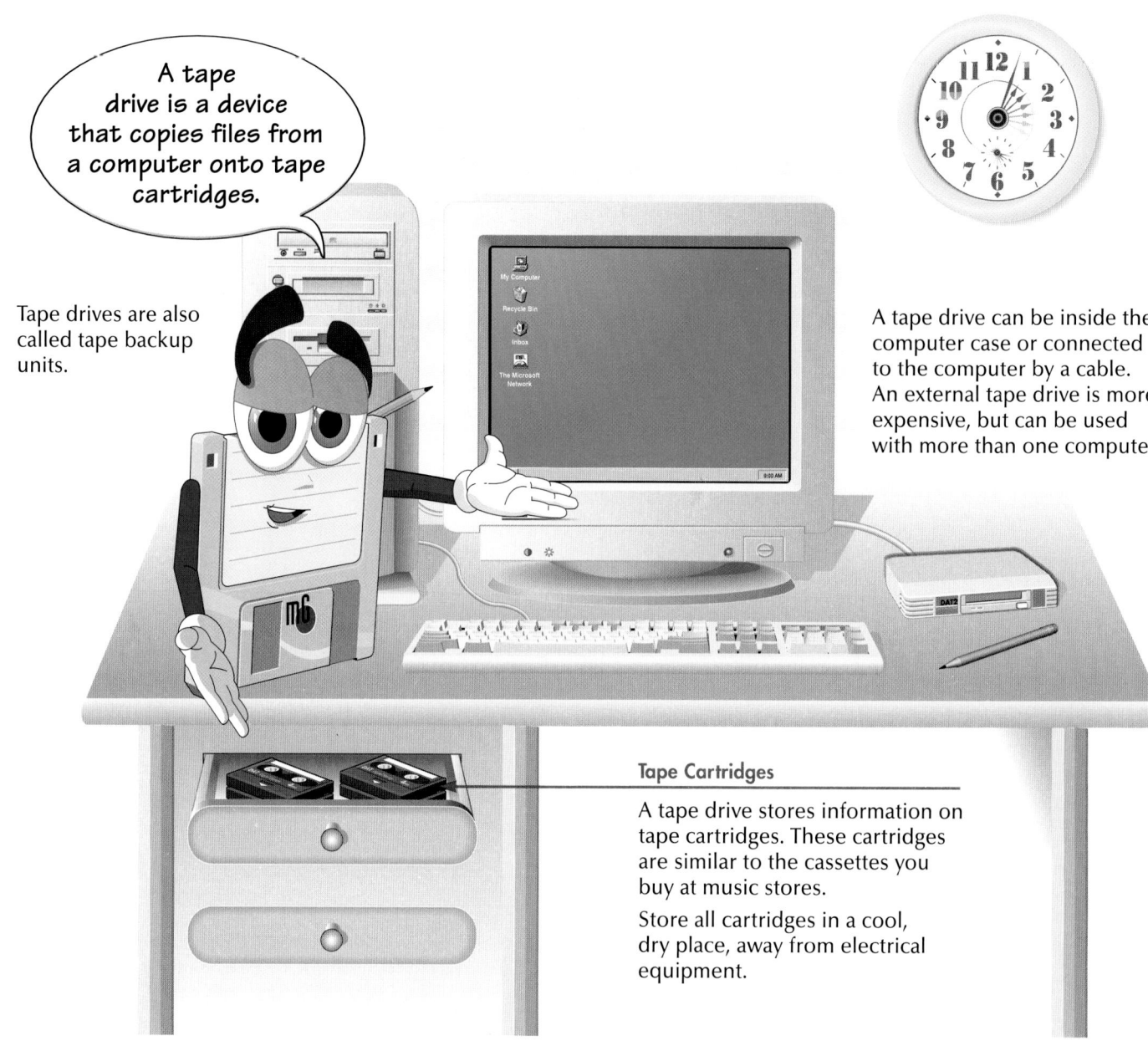

A tape drive is a device that copies files from a computer onto tape cartridges.

Tape drives are also called tape backup units.

A tape drive can be inside the computer case or connected to the computer by a cable. An external tape drive is more expensive, but can be used with more than one computer.

Tape Cartridges

A tape drive stores information on tape cartridges. These cartridges are similar to the cassettes you buy at music stores.

Store all cartridges in a cool, dry place, away from electrical equipment.

TAPE DRIVE APPLICATIONS

Back Up Data

Most people use tape drives to make backup copies of files stored on a computer. This provides extra copies in case the original files are stolen or damaged due to viruses or computer failure. Most people should back up their work every day.

Archive Data

You can copy old or rarely used files from your computer to tape cartridges. You can then remove the files from your computer to provide more storage space.

Transfer Data

You can use a tape drive to transfer large amounts of information between computers. Make sure the person receiving the information uses the same type of tape drive.

BACKUP PROGRAM

> A backup program helps you copy the files stored on your computer to tape cartridges.

Most tape drives come with a backup program specifically designed for use with the tape drive. Windows 95 also includes a backup program.

Schedule Backups

You can set a backup program to run automatically. This lets you schedule a backup at night, when you are not using your computer.

Types of Backups

A full backup will back up all your files. An incremental backup will back up only the files that have changed since the last backup. An incremental backup saves you time when backing up a lot of information.

Compress Data

A backup program can compress, or squeeze together, data you are backing up to double the amount of data you can store on a tape cartridge.

TYPES OF TAPE DRIVES

QIC Drive

A Quarter-Inch Cartridge (QIC) drive is currently the most common type of tape drive. A high-quality QIC drive can store up to 4 GB of data.

Travan Drive

Travan is a new type of tape drive. This drive stores more information and is faster than a QIC drive. A Travan drive also accepts QIC tape cartridges. A high-quality Travan drive can store up to 8 GB of data.

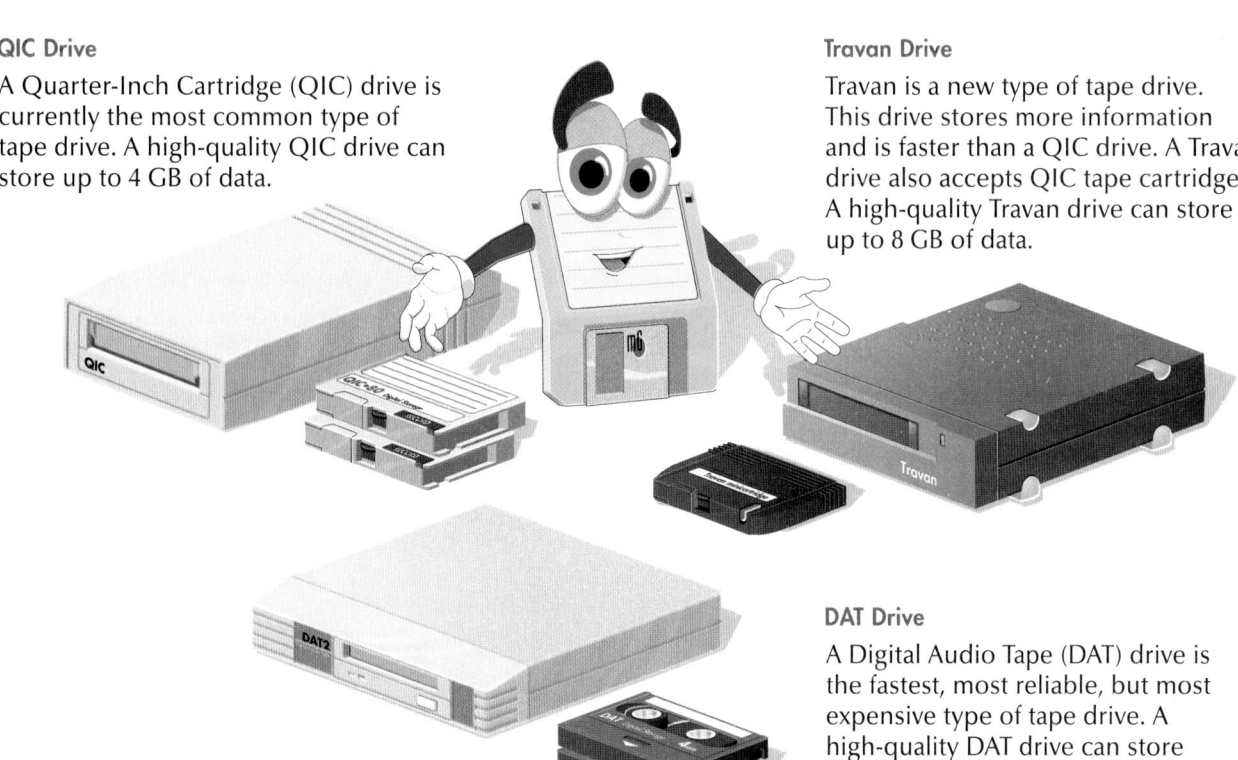

DAT Drive

A Digital Audio Tape (DAT) drive is the fastest, most reliable, but most expensive type of tape drive. A high-quality DAT drive can store up to 10 GB of data.

TAPE CARTRIDGES TIP

Companies often advertise the amount of compressed data a tape cartridge can store. Companies assume that compression will double the amount of information a cartridge can store. This is not always the case.

The amount of information that is actually compressed depends on the type of information you are backing up. For example, a text file will compress significantly more than a graphics file.

CHAPTER 5

PORTABLE COMPUTERS

INTRODUCTION TO PORTABLE COMPUTERS

A portable is a small, lightweight computer that you can easily transport.

A portable computer is also called a laptop or notebook.

You can buy a portable computer with the same capabilities as a desktop computer, although portable computers are more expensive.

A portable computer has a built-in keyboard, pointing device and screen. This eliminates the need for cables to connect these devices to the portable.

ADVANTAGES OF PORTABLES

Travel

A portable computer lets you work when traveling or outdoors. You can also use a portable computer to bring work home instead of staying late at the office.

Presentations

You can bring a portable computer to meetings to present information.

BATTERY

A battery or an electrical outlet can supply the power for a portable computer.

A battery lets you use a portable when no electrical outlets are available.

TYPES OF BATTERIES

There are two main types of batteries—nickel metal hydride (NiMH) and lithium-ion. Lithium-ion is a more expensive, newer battery that is lighter and lasts longer than NiMH.

MONITOR A BATTERY

Most portables display the amount of battery power remaining, either on the screen or on a panel built into the computer.

RECHARGE A BATTERY

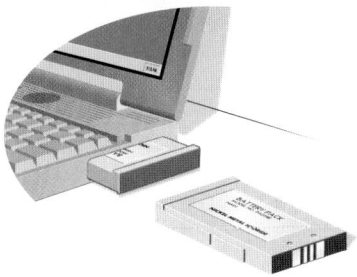

The power supplied by a battery lasts for only a few hours. You must recharge a battery before you can use it again. If you are unable to recharge a battery when traveling, bring an extra battery so you can work for a longer period of time.

SCREEN

The screen on a portable computer uses liquid crystal display (LCD). This is the same type of display found in most digital wristwatches.

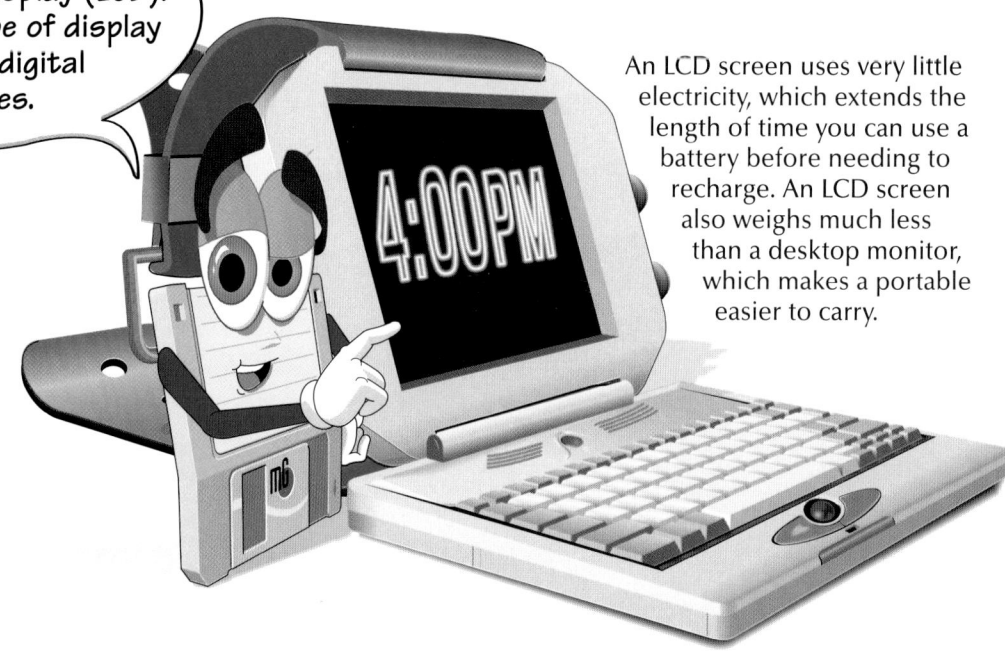

An LCD screen uses very little electricity, which extends the length of time you can use a battery before needing to recharge. An LCD screen also weighs much less than a desktop monitor, which makes a portable easier to carry.

BACKLIGHT

Most portables have an internal light source at the back of the screen. This makes the screen easier to view in poorly lit areas but shortens the length of time you can use a battery before needing to recharge.

POWER A FULL-SIZE MONITOR

Most portables can power both the portable screen and a full-size monitor at the same time. This feature is very useful when delivering presentations.

SCREEN SIZE

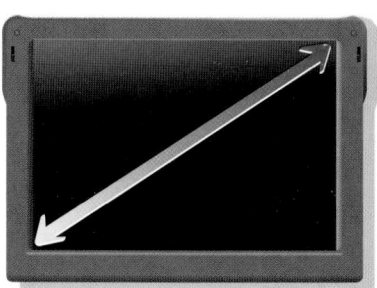

The size of the screen is measured diagonally. Screen sizes range from about 9 to 12 inches.

TYPES OF SCREENS

Passive Matrix

This type of screen is less expensive than an active matrix screen, but is not as bright or rich in color. The lower cost makes a passive matrix screen ideal for routine office tasks.

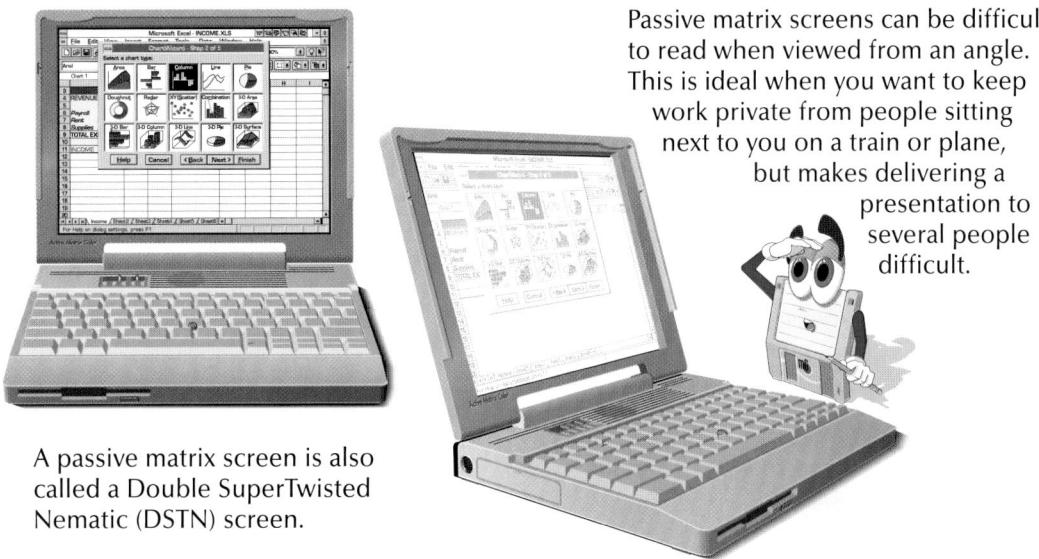

A passive matrix screen is also called a Double SuperTwisted Nematic (DSTN) screen.

Passive matrix screens can be difficult to read when viewed from an angle. This is ideal when you want to keep work private from people sitting next to you on a train or plane, but makes delivering a presentation to several people difficult.

Active Matrix

This type of screen is more expensive, but displays brighter, richer colors than a passive matrix screen.

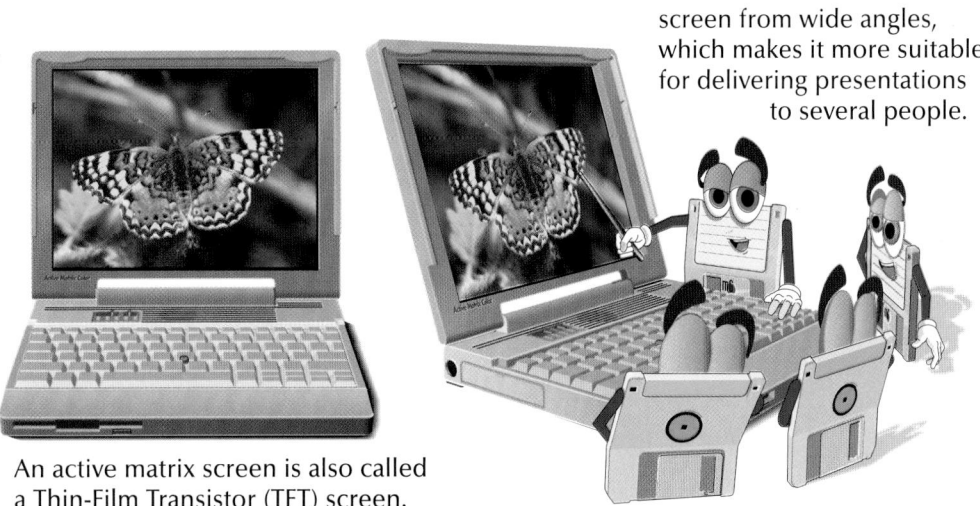

An active matrix screen is also called a Thin-Film Transistor (TFT) screen.

You can view an active matrix screen from wide angles, which makes it more suitable for delivering presentations to several people.

INPUT AND OUTPUT DEVICES

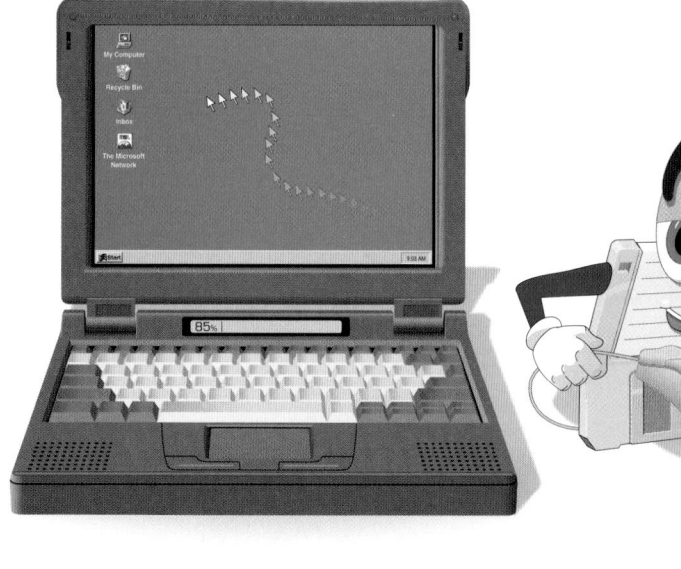

There are several devices that let you move the pointer around the screen of a portable computer.

A mouse is impractical when traveling, since you need a relatively large, flat surface to move the mouse.

Pointing Stick

Many portables have a small, eraser-like device that you push in different directions to move the pointer on the screen.

Trackball

A trackball is an upside-down mouse that remains stationary. You roll the ball with your fingers or palm to move the pointer on the screen. Built-in trackballs on the right side of the keyboard may be awkward for left-handed users.

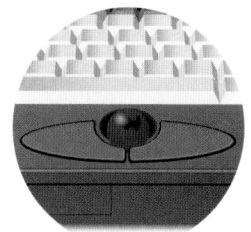

Touchpad

A touchpad is a surface that is sensitive to pressure and motion. When you move your fingertip across the pad, the pointer on the screen moves in the same direction.

KEYBOARD

The keys on a portable keyboard may be small and close together to save space. Before buying a portable, type several paragraphs of text to make sure the keyboard is suitable for you.

Some portable computers have a keyboard that expands to a full-size keyboard.

MODEM

You can buy a portable with a built-in modem or add modem capabilities later. When traveling, a modem lets you connect to the network at work to exchange messages and files.

Many hotel phone systems cannot support modems. Check with hotel management before using your modem.

SOUND CARD AND SPEAKERS

You can buy a portable with a built-in sound card and speakers to play and record sound. This is very useful when you want to use the portable to deliver presentations.

STORAGE DEVICES

HARD DRIVE

The hard drive is the primary device a portable uses to store information. Buy the largest hard drive you can afford. New programs and data will quickly fill a hard drive.

CD-ROM DRIVE

A portable computer may come with a CD-ROM drive to read information stored on compact discs.

Some portables let you replace the CD-ROM drive with another component. These components can include an extra battery to increase the amount of time you can use the portable, a second hard drive for additional storage space or a floppy drive.

FLOPPY DRIVE

Many portables come with a floppy drive to store and retrieve information on floppy disks.

If you will not use a floppy drive very often, you can buy a portable without a floppy drive to reduce the portable's weight. You can then connect the portable to an external floppy drive when necessary.

PROCESSING

CPU

The Central Processing Unit (CPU) is the main chip in a computer. The CPU processes instructions, performs calculations and manages the flow of information through a computer system.

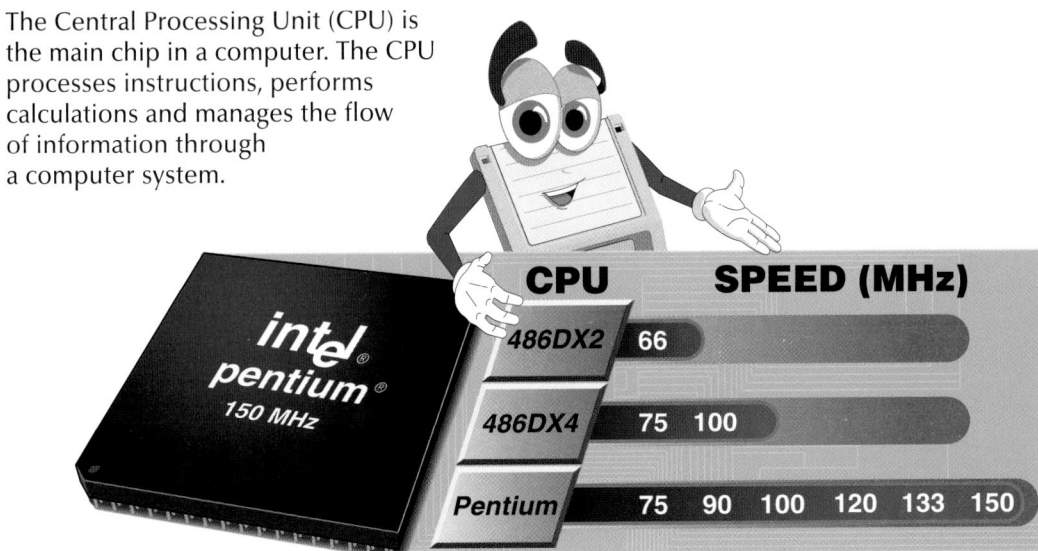

CPU	SPEED (MHz)					
486DX2	66					
486DX4	75	100				
Pentium	75	90	100	120	133	150

This chart shows the CPU chips available for portable computers. Which chip you decide to buy depends on your budget and how you plan to use the computer.

MEMORY

Electronic memory, or RAM, temporarily stores data inside a computer. Memory works like a blackboard that is constantly overwritten with new data. A portable computer running Windows 95 needs at least 8 MB of memory to ensure that programs run smoothly.

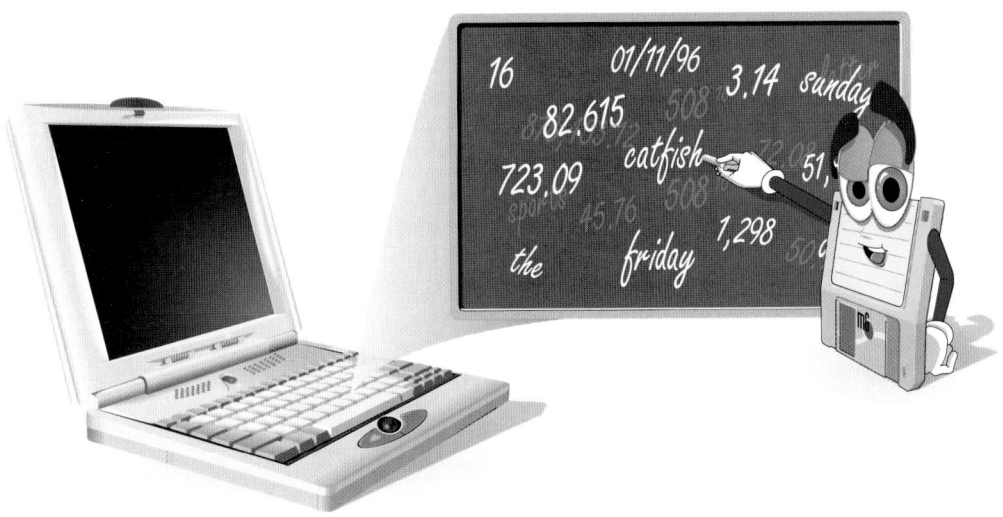

PCMCIA CARD

A PCMCIA Card adds a new capability, such as sound or additional memory, to a portable computer.

PCMCIA stands for Personal Computer Memory Card International Association. A PCMCIA Card is also called a PC Card.

Some PCMCIA Cards provide multiple features. For example, a single PCMCIA Card can provide networking and modem capabilities.

TYPES OF PCMCIA CARDS

A PCMCIA Card is a lightweight device about the size of a credit card. There are three types of PCMCIA Cards—Type I, Type II and Type III. Type I is the thinnest card, while Type III is the thickest. Each type of card can vary in the features it offers.

PCMCIA SLOT

You insert a PCMCIA Card into a slot on a portable computer. Most portable computers have a PCMCIA slot that can accept two Type I or Type II PCMCIA Cards or one Type III PCMCIA Card.

USE A PORTABLE AT WORK

Infrared Port

Some portable computers have an infrared port to share information without using cables to physically connect to another computer or device. Infrared ports are commonly used for connecting a portable computer to a printer or network.

Port Replicator

A port replicator lets you connect many devices, such as a printer, modem and mouse, to a portable at once. After you connect a portable to a port replicator, you can use all the devices attached to the port replicator without having to attach each device individually.

Docking Station

A docking station lets you connect many devices to a portable at once. A docking station can also provide additional features, such as a CD-ROM drive, networking capabilities and a full-sized monitor and keyboard.

After you connect a portable to a docking station, you can use all the features found on the docking station.

Endnotes

1. Henry Smith, Helping th[e]
   (Los Angeles: Devries, 199[6])

2. K.L. Johnston, World[...]
   (New York: Matwey, 19[...])

3. Michelle Lucas, Th[...]
   (Philadelphia: Purch[...])

4. William Jones, [...]
   (Los Angeles: De[...])

5. D.S. Davies, [...]
   (New York: M[...])

6. Susan Hill[...]
   (Philadelph[...])

GLOBAL REPORT

Seventy-five percent of the World's people live in the Third World. These nations supply the developed nations with a multitude of raw materials and natural resources, and also buy many of our exports (40% of U.S. exports are bought by the Third World). Clearly the lives of the people in the developed and underdeveloped worlds are unavoidably interre[...]

underdeveloped countries (UDC) is that since the Colonial period, exploitation of their arable land has rapidly increased. Companies from the developed countries (DC) are blamed for abusing the land, but the farmers and locals are often guilty as well. Seventy-five percent of the energy[...] the UDC's[...]

Save the World Inc.

NEWSLETTER - JUNE 1996

[1]Henry [...]
(Los Ang[...])

[2]K.L. Joh[...]
(New York[...])

[3]Michelle Lu[...]
(Philadelphia[...])

Seventy-five percent of the World's people live in the Third World. These nations supply the developed nations with a multitude of raw materials and natural resources, and also buy many of our exports, (40% of U.S. exports are bought by the Third World). Clearly the lives of the people in the developed and underdeveloped worlds are unavoidably interrelated. It is for this reason that it is important for the rich nations to study the problems in other countries and help them to overcome them. One major problem in most underdeveloped countries (UDC), is that since the Colonial period, exploitation of their[...]

eventually whole forests disappear. The land then no longer has anything holding it together. This results in soil erosion and loss of water retaining abilities.

Development in the Western sense is to industrialize your economy. It is essential for the Third World to develop their production techniques, especially in agriculture, in order to compete effectively on the World Markets. This kind of development, however, requires not only costly machinery, but expensive fossil fuels for operation.

David C. Thompson
President
Dynamic Advertising Inc.
1223 Lincoln Ave.
New York, N.Y.
10023

Dear Mr. Thompson,

I would like to take this opportunity to congratulate you and your company for winning First Prize in the 1996 Logo Design Contest. It gives me the greatest pleasure to inform you that the Judging Committee's decision was unanimous. Your entry was clearly the best among the hundreds of outstanding entries we received this year.

Enclosed please find a copy of the Judging Committee's remarks. This report states that "the logo designed by Dynamic Advertising Inc. serves to enhance the company's image through the creative use of colors and modern design principles."

The award will be presented on August 20 at the International Design Institute's annual banquet. We hope to see you then.

Once again, please accept my congratulations.

Sincerely,

Karen Davis
Chairperson
Judging Committee

261 Main St.
Chicago, IL.
60611

(555) 555-1241
(555) 555-1210

Goals for the end of the year:

- Pay off the mortgage
- Save money for a vacation
- Finish painting the house
- Join a health club
- Read mo[re]
- Do volu[...]
  the comm[unity]

Recipe:

1. Preheat oven to 300°F
2. Grate 1 cup of cheese
3. Dice 1/4 cup of onions
4. Slice 1/2 a red pepper into thin strips
5. Add cheese, onions and red pepper to meat sauce
6. Bake for 20 minutes

Ready to start that report? Browse through this chapter to discover how application software can help you get the job done.

APPLICATION SOFTWARE

INTRODUCTION TO APPLICATION SOFTWARE

Application software helps you accomplish specific tasks.

You can use application software to write letters, manage your finances, draw pictures, play games and much more.

Application software is also called software, an application or a program.

GET SOFTWARE

You can buy software at computer stores. There are also thousands of programs available on the Internet.

INSTALL SOFTWARE

Software you buy at a computer store comes on a single CD-ROM disc or several floppy disks. Before you can use the software, you must install, or copy, the contents of the disc or disks to your computer. Using a CD-ROM disc is a fast method of installing software.

SOFTWARE VERSION

Software developers and manufacturers constantly make corrections (called bug-fixes) and add new features to the software they create. When a manufacturer releases updated software, the software is given a new version number. This helps people distinguish new versions of the software from older versions.

BUNDLED SOFTWARE

Bundled software is software that comes with a new computer system or device, such as a printer. Companies often include bundled software to let you start using the new equipment right away. For example, new computer systems usually come with word processing, spreadsheet and graphics programs.

GET HELP

Most software comes with a built-in help feature and printed documentation to help you learn to use the software. You can also buy computer books with detailed, step-by-step instructions at computer or book stores.

WORD PROCESSOR

A word processor helps you create professional-looking documents quickly and efficiently.

Popular word processing programs include Microsoft Word, Corel WordPerfect and Lotus Word Pro.

WORD PROCESSING HIGHLIGHTS

Documents

You can create documents such as letters, reports, manuals, newsletters and brochures. You can style documents to make them attractive or add pictures.

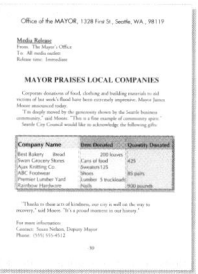

Tables

You can create tables to organize information. You can also add colors and borders to enhance the appearance of tables.

Mail Merge

Word processors offer a merge feature that lets you quickly produce personalized letters, envelopes and mailing labels for each person on a mailing list.

WORD PROCESSING BASICS

Scroll

If you create a long document, the computer screen cannot display all the text at the same time. You must scroll up or down to view and edit other parts of the document.

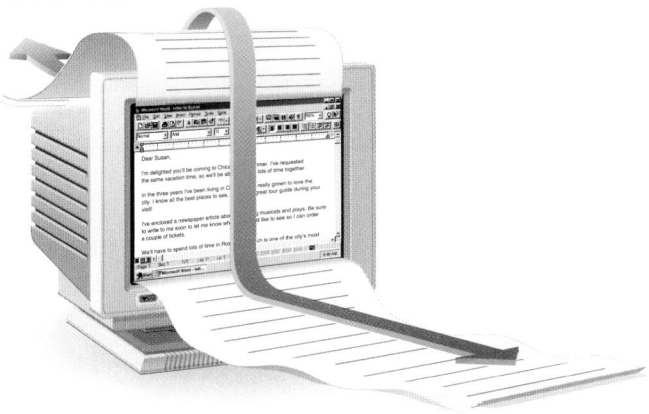

Word Wrap

A word processor automatically moves text you type to the next line. This is called word wrapping. When typing text, you only need to press **Enter** when you want to start a new paragraph.

When you use a word processor to type a letter, the text automatically wraps to the next line as you type.

Insertion Point

The flashing line on a screen is called the insertion point. It indicates where the text you type will appear in the document.

Select Text

Before performing certain tasks, you must select the text you want to work with. Selected text appears highlighted on the screen.

I'm delighted you'll be coming to Chicago this summer.

EDIT A DOCUMENT

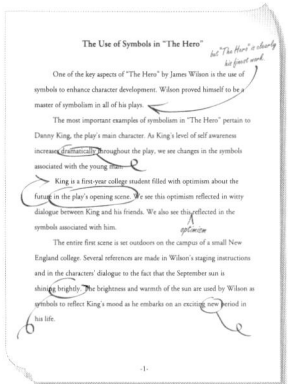

Edit Text

After typing text in a document, you can easily add new text, delete text or move text to a new location. A word processor also remembers the last changes you made to a document and lets you undo, or cancel, the changes.

Search and Replace

You can locate and replace every occurrence of a word or phrase in a document. This is ideal if you have frequently misspelled a name.

Spelling and Grammar

A word processor includes a spell checker to find and correct spelling errors in a document. Some word processors will correct common spelling errors as you type.

Word processors also include a grammar checker to find grammar, punctuation and stylistic errors.

Thesaurus

A thesaurus helps you add variety to your writing. This feature lets you replace a word in a document with one that is more suitable.

FONT

A font refers to the design and size of characters in a document.

You will usually have all the fonts you need to create attractive documents. If you want more choices when creating documents, you can purchase additional fonts at most computer stores.

A font consists of three elements: typeface, type size and type style.

Arial
Brush Script MT
Bodoni
Courier New
Times New Roman

10 point
12 point
14 point
18 point
24 point

Bold
Italic
SMALL CAPS
~~Strikethrough~~
XXX^{Superscript}
XXX_{Subscript}
<u>Underline</u>

Typeface
Typeface refers to the design of characters.

Type Size
Type size refers to the size of characters and is measured in points. Most business documents use 10 or 12 point type. There are approximately 72 points in one inch.

Type Style
Type style refers to the appearance of characters.

FORMAT A PARAGRAPH

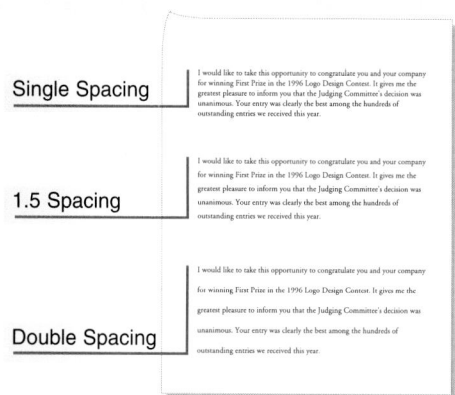

Single Spacing

1.5 Spacing

Double Spacing

Line Spacing

You can make a document easier to read by changing the amount of space between the lines of text.

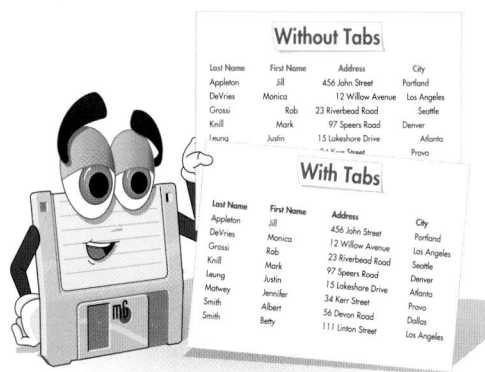

Tabs

You can use tabs to line up columns of information in a document. Use tabs instead of spaces to line up columns of text to ensure that a document will print correctly.

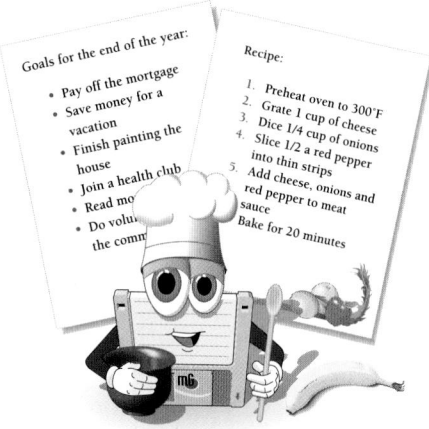

List

You can separate items in a list by beginning each item with a bullet or number. Bullets are useful for items in no particular order, such as a list of goals. Numbers are useful for items in a specific order, such as instructions for a recipe.

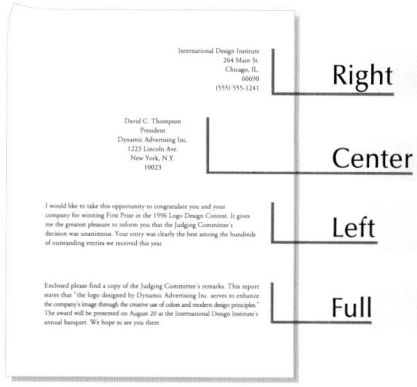

Right

Center

Left

Full

Text Alignment

You can enhance the appearance of a document by aligning paragraphs in different ways.

FORMAT A PAGE

Margin

A margin is the space between text and an edge of the paper. You can change the margin settings to adjust the length of a document or accommodate letterhead or other specialty paper.

Header and Footer

You can add a header or footer to each page of a document to display information such as the date or company name. A header appears at the top of each page. A footer appears at the bottom of each page.

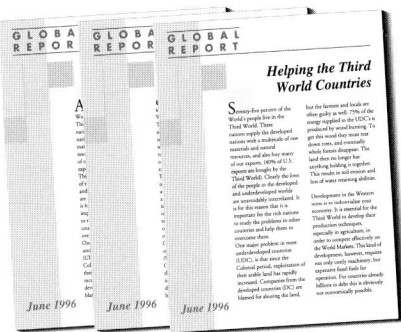

Footnote and Endnote

Footnotes and endnotes provide additional information about text in a document. A footnote appears at the bottom of the page that contains the footnote number. An endnote appears at the end of the document.

Page Number

A word processor can number the pages in a document. You can specify the position and style of the page numbers.

SPREADSHEET

A spreadsheet program helps you manage personal and business finances.

Popular spreadsheet programs include Lotus 1-2-3 and Microsoft Excel.

SPREADSHEET APPLICATIONS

Manage Finances

You can use a spreadsheet program to perform calculations, analyze data and present information.

Manage Data in a List

A spreadsheet program lets you store a large collection of information such as a mailing or product list. Spreadsheet programs include tools for organizing, managing, sorting and retrieving data.

If you want greater control over a list stored on your computer, use a database program. Database programs are specifically designed to manage a list of data.

SPREADSHEET BASICS

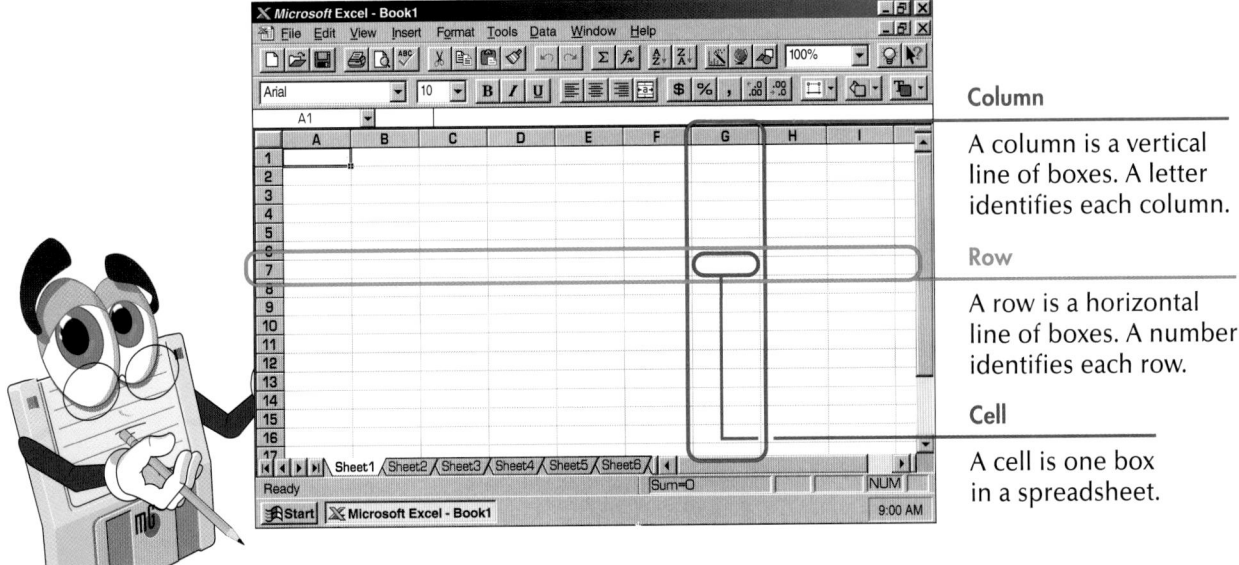

Column

A column is a vertical line of boxes. A letter identifies each column.

Row

A row is a horizontal line of boxes. A number identifies each row.

Cell

A cell is one box in a spreadsheet.

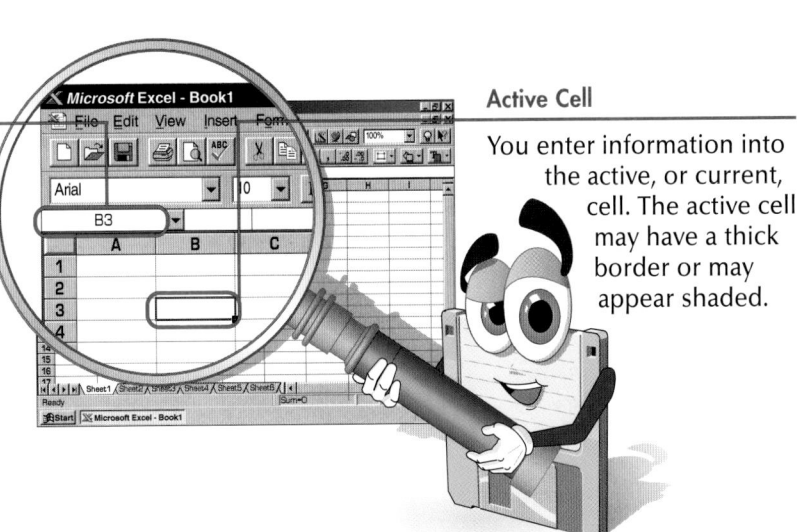

Cell Reference

A cell reference or cell address defines the location of each cell in a spreadsheet. It consists of a column letter followed by a row number.

Active Cell

You enter information into the active, or current, cell. The active cell may have a thick border or may appear shaded.

FORMULA

> A formula helps you calculate and analyze data in a spreadsheet.

Spreadsheet programs perform calculations in the following order:

1. Exponents (^)
2. Multiply (*) and Divide (/)
3. Add (+) and Subtract (–)

When entering formulas, use cell references (example: A1+A2) instead of actual data (example: 10+20) whenever possible.

	A
1	10
2	20
3	30
4	40
5	100

■ This cell contains the result of the formula:

=A1+A2+A3+A4

=10+20+30+40

=100

	A
1	30
2	40
3	100
4	50
5	72

■ This cell contains the result of the formula:

=A1+A2+A3/A4

=30+40+100/50

=72

FORMULA TIPS

Automatic Recalculation

If you change a number used in a formula, you do not have to manually redo all the calculations. A spreadsheet program will automatically redo the calculations and display the new results.

	30
Unit 1	70
Unit 2	45
Unit 3	
Total	**145**

This feature is very useful if you want to evaluate several possible scenarios, such as how different interest rates affect your mortgage payments. You can change one number and instantly see the effects on the rest of the data.

Using Parentheses

If you use parentheses ( ) in a formula, a spreadsheet program will calculate the data inside the parentheses first.

	A
1	10
2	70
3	50
4	20
5	220

■ This cell contains the result of the formula:

=A1*(A2-A3)+A4

=10*(70-50)+20

=220

Copy a Formula

After entering a formula in a spreadsheet, you can save time by copying the formula to other cells. A spreadsheet program will automatically change the cell references in the new formulas for you.

	A	B	C
1	10	20	5
2	20	30	10
3	30	40	20
4	60	90	35

=A1+A2+A3	⇒	=B1+B2+B3	=C1+C2+C3

Original formula   Copied formulas

FUNCTION

A function is a ready-to-use formula that helps you perform specialized calculations.

The SUM function adds a list of numbers.

■ This cell contains the result of the function:

=SUM(A1:A4)

=A1+A2+A3+A4

=10+20+30+40

=100

The AVERAGE function calculates the average value of a list of numbers.

■ This cell contains the result of the function:

=AVERAGE(A1:A4)

=(A1+A2+A3+A4)/4

=(30+40+20+10)/4

=25

The MAX function finds the largest value in a list of numbers.

■ This cell contains the result of the function:

=MAX(A1:A4)

=70

Column Width and Row Height

You can change the width of columns and the height of rows to fit the data.

Edit Data

After entering data in a spreadsheet, you can add new data, delete data or move data to a new location. A spreadsheet program also remembers the last change you made and lets you undo, or cancel, the change.

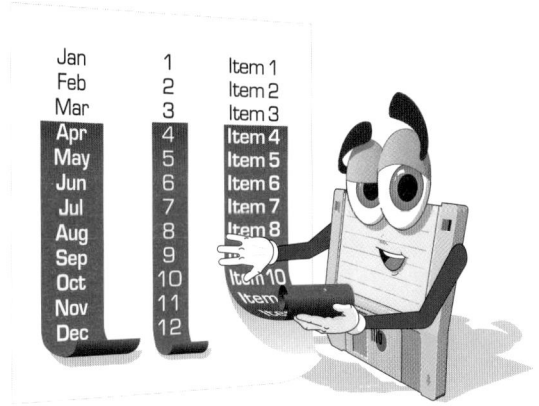

Complete a Series

A spreadsheet program can save you time by completing a series of numbers, text or time periods for you.

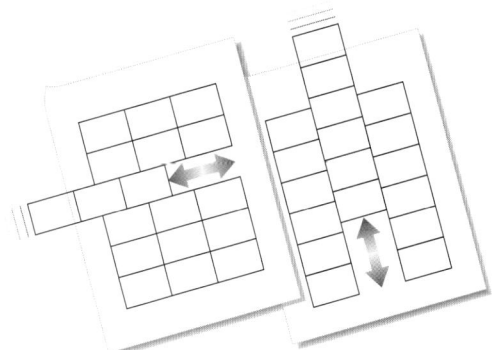

Rows and Columns

You can insert rows and columns to add new data. You can also delete rows and columns to remove data you do not need.

FORMAT A SPREADSHEET

Font

You can change the design and size of characters to make a spreadsheet more appealing.

Number Appearance

You can change the look of numbers in a spreadsheet. A spreadsheet program offers many different ways to display numbers to make them easier to read and identify.

Borders, Shading and Color

You can add borders, shading and color to improve the appearance of a spreadsheet.

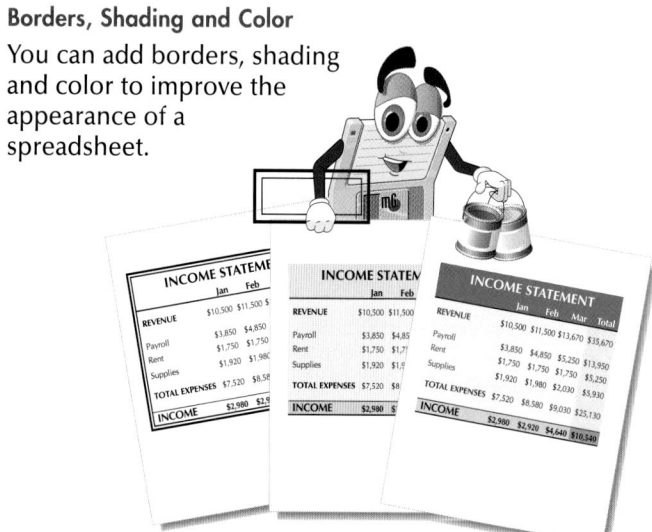

Data Alignment

You can change the position of data in each cell of a spreadsheet. For example, you can center all titles and right align all numbers.

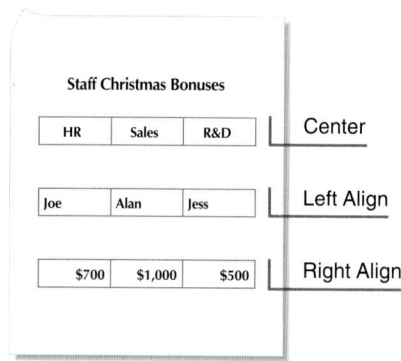

CHART

A chart lets you graphically display the data in a spreadsheet.

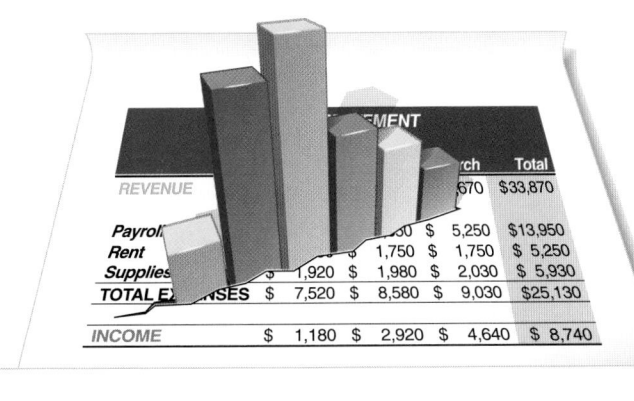

After creating a chart, you can select a new type of chart that will better suit the data.

Parts of a Chart

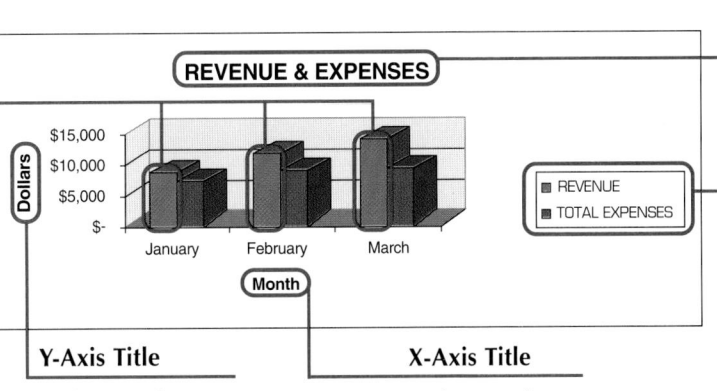

Data Series

A group of related data representing one row or column from the spreadsheet. Each data series is a specific color, pattern or symbol.

Chart Title

Identifies the subject of the chart.

Legend

Labels the color, pattern or symbol used for each data series in the chart.

Y-Axis Title

Indicates the unit of measure used in the chart.

X-Axis Title

Indicates the categories used in the chart.

DATABASE

A database program helps you manage large collections of information.

Database programs are commonly used to manage mailing lists, phone directories, product listings and payroll information.

Popular database programs include Microsoft Access and Borland dBASE

DATABASE APPLICATIONS

Store Data
You can use a database program to keep large collections of information organized and up-to-date.

Create Reports
You can use the information in a database to create reports and presentations.

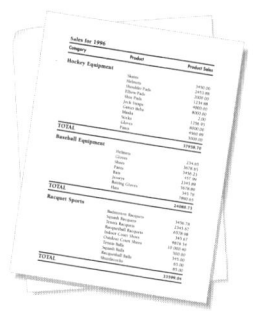

Analyze Data
You can perform calculations on the information in a database. You can then analyze the results to make quick, accurate and informed decisions.

MANAGE INFORMATION

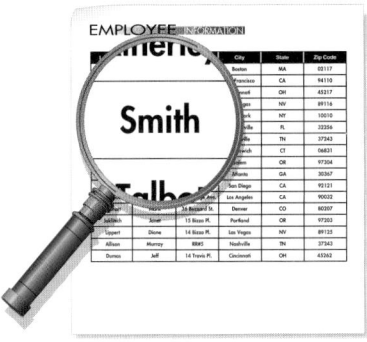

Sort

You can change the order of information in a database. For example, you can alphabetically sort all employees by last name.

Find

You can locate specific information in a database. For example, you can search for the name of a particular employee.

Query

You can create a query, which asks a database program to find information that meets certain criteria, or conditions. This lets you gather information of interest to you.

For example, a query can gather information on employees who sold more than 1000 units of product A last month. You can use the results of a query to create a report.

DATABASE continued

PARTS OF A DATABASE

Table

A table is a collection of information about a specific topic, such as a mailing or product list. A database can consist of one or more tables.

Client Addresses : Table					
Last Name	**First Name**	**Address**	**City**	**State**	**Zip Code**
Smith	John	258 Linton Ave.	New York	NY	10010-
Lang	Diane	50 Tree Lane	Boston	MA	02117-
Oram	Derek	68 Cacker Ave.	San Francisco	CA	94110-
Gray	Russel	1 Hollywood Blvd.	Cincinnati	OH	45217-
Atherley	Peter	47 Cosby Ave.	Las Vegas	NV	89116-
Talbot	Mark	26 Arnold Cres.	Jacksonville	FL	32256-
Coleman	Duane	401 Idon Dr.	Nashville	TN	37243-
Sanvido	Dean	16 Hoover Cres.	Greenwich	CT	06831-
Slater	Mark	468 Starewell Rd.	Salem	MA	97304-
Pozeg	Dan	10 Heldon St.	Atlanta	GA	30367-
Hretchka	Steve	890 Apple St.	San Diego	CA	92121-
Gombocz	Sandor	18 Goulage Ave.	Los Angeles	CA	90032-
Boshart	Mark	36 Buzzard St.	Boston	MA	02118-
Jaklitsch	Janet	15 Bizzo Pl.	New York	NY	10020-

Record: 1 of 14

Field

A field is a single piece of information in a record. For example, a field could be the first name of a client.

Field Name

A field name identifies the information contained in a field.

Record

A record is a collection of information about one person, place or thing. For example, a record could contain the name and address of a client.

FORM

You can use a form to help you enter data into a database. A form has boxes that clearly show you where to enter data.

Addresses	
Address ID	1
First Name	John
Last Name	Smith
Address	258 Linton Ave.
City	New York
State/Province	NY
Postal Code	10010-
Country	US
Spouse Name	Kristin
Home Phone	(212) 555-1234
Work Phone	(212) 555-6789
Work Extension	507
Fax Number	(212) 555-6790

Preview Fact Sheet... Dial... Page: 1 2

Record: 1 of 1

TYPES OF DATABASES

Flat File Database

A flat file database stores information in a single table.

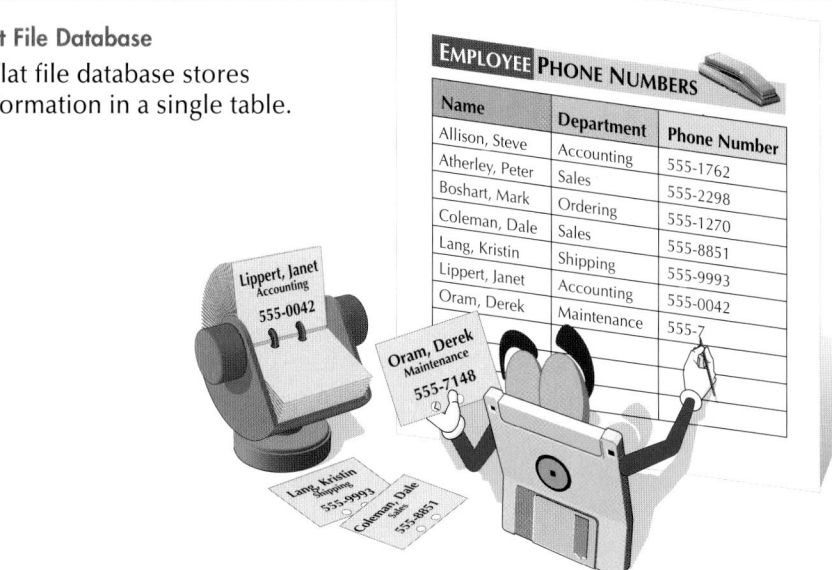

Name	Department	Phone Number
Allison, Steve	Accounting	555-1762
Atherley, Peter	Sales	555-2298
Boshart, Mark	Ordering	555-1270
Coleman, Dale	Sales	555-8851
Lang, Kristin	Shipping	555-9993
Lippert, Janet	Accounting	555-0042
Oram, Derek	Maintenance	555-7

A flat file database is easy to set up and learn. This type of database is ideal for simple lists, such as phone number and mailing lists.

Relational Database

A relational database lets you take information from different sources and organize the information in a single database.

CLIENT ADDRESSES

Name	Address	City	State
Atherley, Peter	15 River St.	La Jolia	CA
Coleman, Dale	82 15th Ave.	New York	NY
Lang, Kristin	24 Ladner Cr.	Cleveland	OH
Oram, Derek	7 Pindar Rd.	Seattle	WA
Sanvido, Dean	60 Norfolk St.	Salem	NH
Smith, John	31 6th Ave.	New York	NY
Talbot, Mark	116 West St.	Marietta	GA

ORDER INFORMATION

#	Product	Quantity	Name
1	C28505	30	Smith, John
2	C48851	100	Oram, Derek
3	C33709	300	Atherley, Peter
4	C40287	25	Smith, John
5	C58209	150	Coleman, Dale
6	C48851	20	Lang, Kristin
7	C33709	35	Sanvido, Dean

INVENTORY

Product	Price	In Stock
C20595	$80.00	12468
C28505	$20.00	1469
C29858	$30.00	50277
C33709	$45.00	6588
C40287	$19.99	206
C48851	$14.99	995
C58209	$79.00	50

A relational database stores information in two or more tables. Each table contains information on a different topic, such as client addresses, order information or inventory.

The tables in a relational database are related, or linked. If you change the information in one table, the same information will automatically change in all other tables. This makes updating fast and accurate.

A relational database is powerful and flexible, but difficult to set up and learn. This type of database is ideal for invoicing, accounting and inventory.

APPLICATION SUITE

An application suite is a collection of programs sold together in one package.

ADVANTAGES

Cost
Buying programs as part of an application suite costs less than buying each program individually.

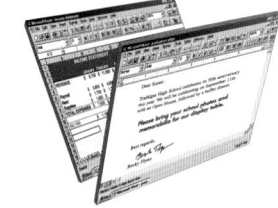

Easy to Use
Programs in an application suite share a common design and work in a similar way. Once you learn one program, you can easily learn the others.

DISADVANTAGE

Since all the programs in an application suite come from the same manufacturer, you may not get the best combination of features for your needs. Make sure you evaluate all the programs in an application suite before making your purchase.

APPLICATION SUITE PROGRAMS

Most application suites include four types of programs. Some application suites also offer additional programs, such as a scheduling program that lets you keep track of appointments.

Word Processing Program

A word processing program lets you create documents, such as letters and reports.

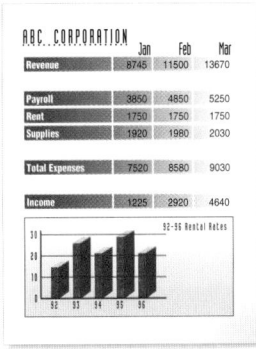

Spreadsheet Program

A spreadsheet program lets you manage and analyze financial information.

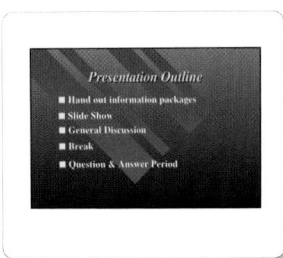

Presentation Program

A presentation program lets you design presentations.

Database Program

A database program lets you manage large collections of information. The database program may only be included in higher-priced versions of the suite.

POPULAR APPLICATION SUITES

Microsoft Office is the most popular application suite.

Other application suites include Corel WordPerfect Suite and Lotus SmartSuite.

OPERATING SYSTEMS

INTRODUCTION TO OPERATING SYSTEMS

An operating system is the software that controls the overall activity of a computer.

An operating system ensures that all parts of a computer system work together smoothly and efficiently.

OPERATING SYSTEM FUNCTIONS

Control Hardware

An operating system controls the different parts of a computer system and enables all the parts to work together.

Run Application Software

An operating system runs application software, such as Microsoft Word and Lotus 1-2-3.

Manage Information

An operating system provides ways to manage and organize information stored on a computer. You can use an operating system to sort, copy, move, delete or view files.

POPULAR OPERATING SYSTEMS

MS-DOS

MS-DOS stands for Microsoft Disk Operating System. MS-DOS displays lines of text on the screen. You perform tasks by typing short commands.

Windows

Windows displays a graphical screen. You use a mouse to perform tasks.

Windows is a Graphical User Interface (GUI, pronounced "gooey"). A GUI allows you to use pictures instead of text commands to perform tasks. This makes Windows easier to use than MS-DOS.

PLATFORM

A platform refers to the type of operating system used by a computer, such as MS-DOS or Windows. Programs used on one platform will not usually work on another platform. For example, you cannot use Word for Windows on a computer running only MS-DOS.

MS-DOS

MS-DOS is an operating system that performs tasks using text commands you enter.

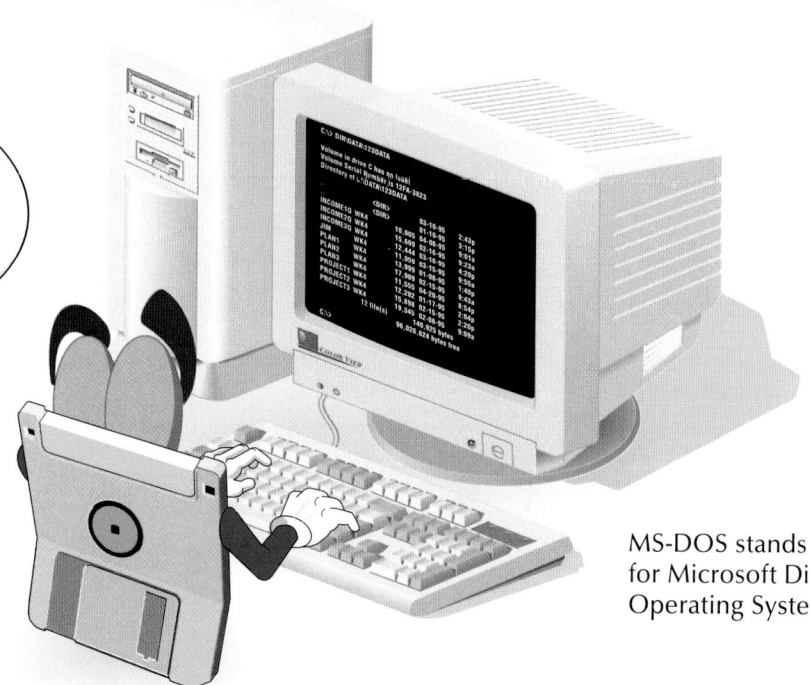

MS-DOS stands for Microsoft Disk Operating System.

ENTER A COMMAND

Command Prompt

The command prompt (C:\>) tells you that MS-DOS is ready to accept a command.

Command

You enter a command to perform a task or start a program. A single command can usually tell the computer what you want to accomplish.

Cursor

The cursor is the flashing line on the screen. The cursor indicates where the text you type will appear.

FILE ORGANIZATION

Like folders in a filing cabinet, MS-DOS uses directories to organize the data stored on a computer.

The root directory (C:\) is the main directory. All other directories are located within this directory.

A path describes the location of a file.

■ The path for this file is c:\letters\personal\john.let

FILE NAME

When you store a file on a computer, you must give the file a name. An MS-DOS file name cannot contain any spaces. A file name consists of a name and an extension, separated by a period.

The name describes the contents of a file and can have up to eight characters.

The extension identifies the type of file and consists of three characters.

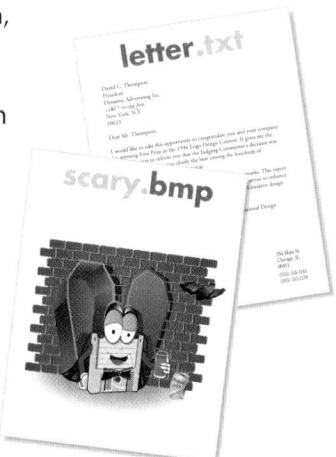

UTILITIES

MS-DOS 6.0 and later versions include special programs, called utilities, to protect files and optimize a computer. For example, one program finds and repairs disk errors.

WINDOWS 3.1

Windows 3.1 works with MS-DOS to control the overall activity of a computer.

Windows 3.1 is not a true operating system since it needs MS-DOS to operate.

A mouse is essential when using Windows.

SELECT A COMMAND

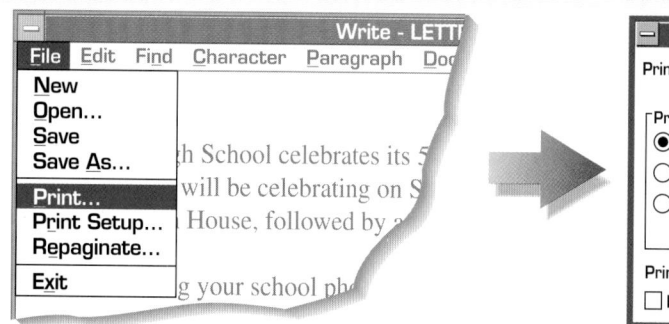

Menu

A menu lists related commands. You select a command from a menu to accomplish a task. For example, the **Print** command lets you produce a paper copy of a document.

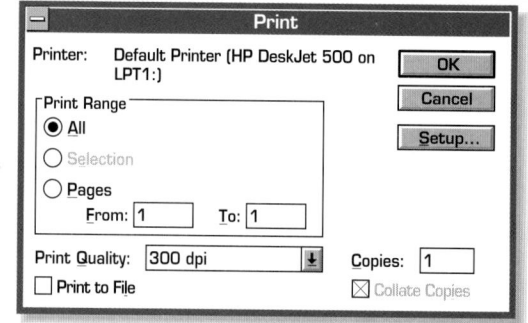

Dialog Box

When you select a command, a dialog box may appear. A dialog box lets you select options before carrying out a command. For example, the Print dialog box lets you choose which pages you want to print.

THE WINDOWS 3.1 SCREEN

Windows 3.1 displays pictures on the screen to help you perform tasks. This makes Windows 3.1 easier to use than MS-DOS.

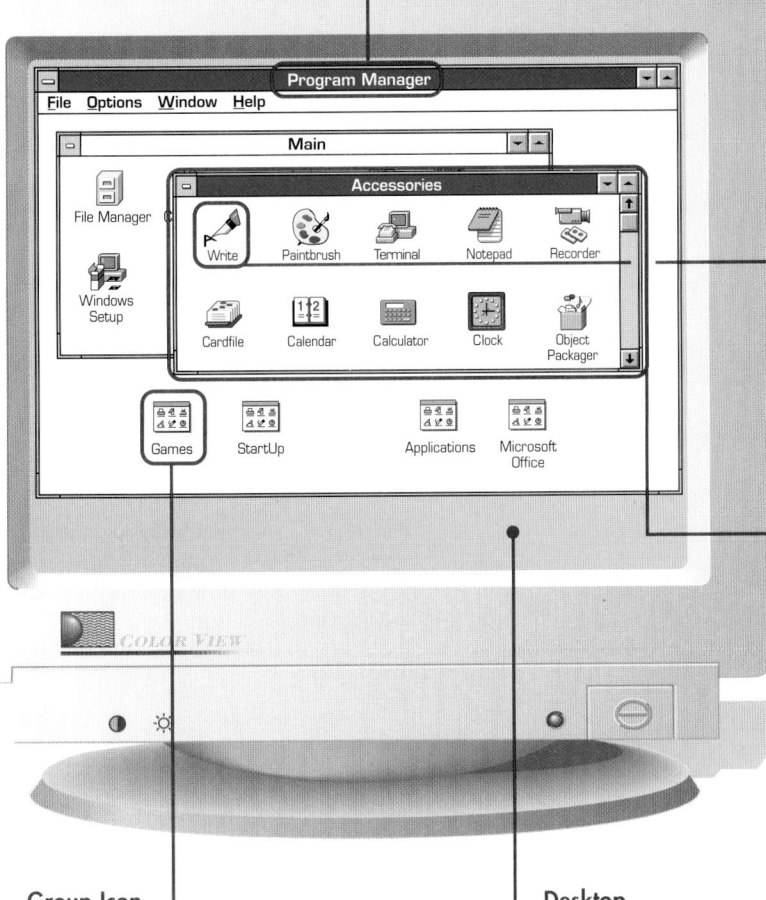

Program Manager

The Program Manager is the control center where you start programs. The Program Manager appears on the screen each time you start Windows 3.1.

Program Icon

A program icon lets you start a program, such as a word processor. An icon is a small picture that represents an object, such as a program.

Window

A window is a rectangle that displays information on the screen. Each window has a title bar that displays the name of the window (example: Accessories).

Group Icon

A group icon contains program icons. For example, the Games group icon contains several games.

Desktop

The desktop is the background area of the screen.

WINDOWS 3.1 FEATURES

Move or Size a Window

You can move a window to a different location on a screen. You can also change the size of a window to display more of its contents.

Control Panel

The Control Panel lets you change the way Windows 3.1 looks and acts. For example, you can change the colors displayed on the screen.

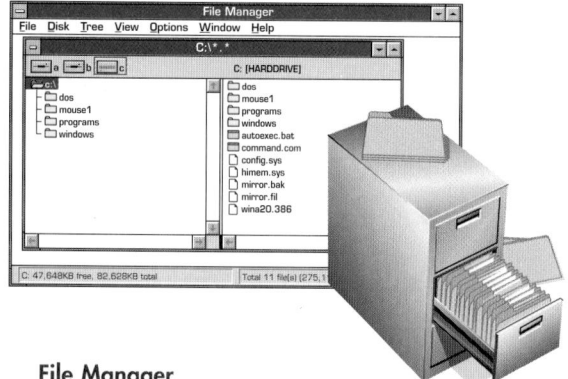

File Manager

The File Manager lets you view and organize all the files stored on a computer. Windows 3.1 uses directories to organize information, just as you would use folders to organize papers in a filing cabinet.

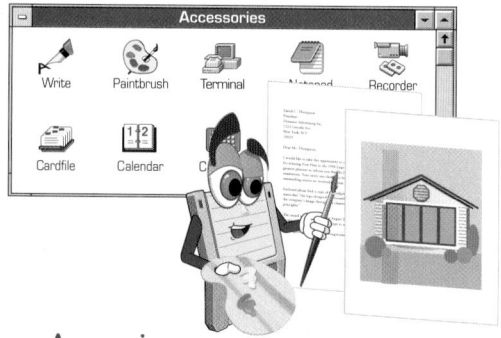

Accessories

Windows 3.1 provides several accessories, or mini-programs, that let you accomplish simple tasks, such as writing letters and drawing pictures.

WORK WITH MULTIPLE PROGRAMS

Windows 3.1 lets you run several programs at the same time and switch between the programs. For example, while writing a letter, you can switch to another program to check your sales figures.

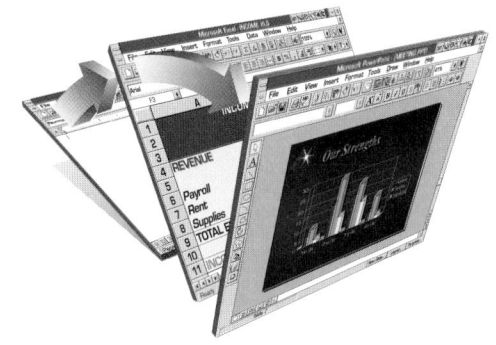

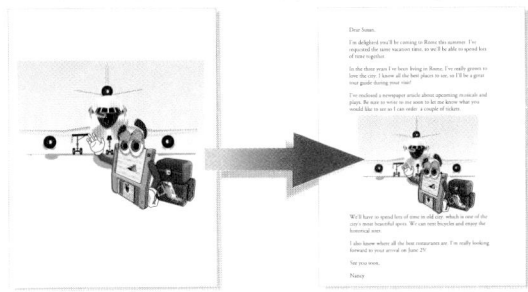

You can easily exchange information between programs in Windows 3.1. For example, you can place a drawing in a letter.

WINDOWS FOR WORKGROUPS 3.11

Windows for Workgroups (WfWG) 3.11 is a more powerful version of Windows 3.1. Like Windows 3.1, this program is not a true operating system since it needs MS-DOS to operate.

Windows for Workgroups 3.11 lets you share files and printers with other computers connected to a network and includes programs for electronic mail and scheduling.

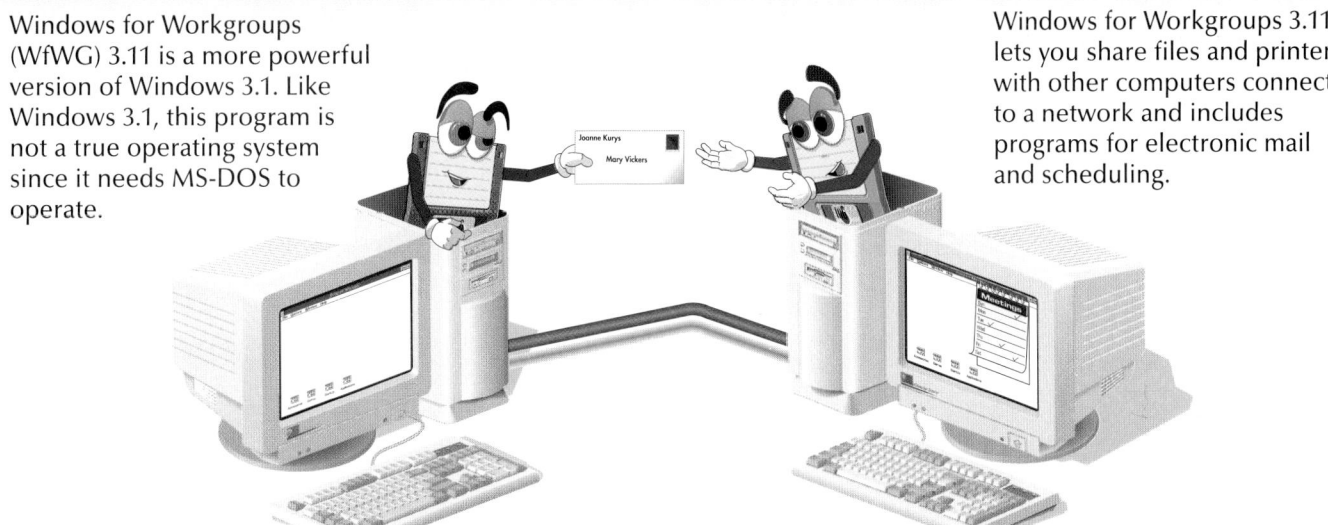

WINDOWS 95

Windows 95 is the successor of Windows 3.1. This operating system is more graphical and easier to use than Windows 3.1.

Windows 95 is a true operating system because it does not need MS-DOS to operate.

Window

A window is a rectangle that displays information on the screen. Each window has a title bar that displays the name of the window (example: My Computer).

My Computer

My Computer lets you browse through all the folders and documents stored on a computer.

Recycle Bin

The Recycle Bin stores all the documents you delete and allows you to recover them later.

Start Button

The Start button lets you quickly access programs and documents.

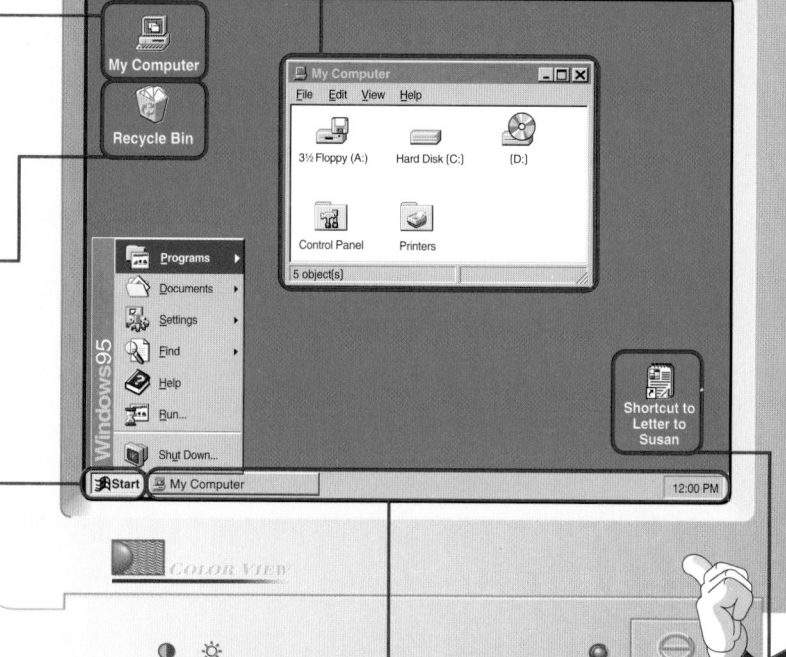

Taskbar

The taskbar contains the Start button and displays the name of each open window on the screen.

Shortcut

A shortcut provides a quick way to open a document or program you use regularly.

WINDOWS 95 FEATURES

Customize Windows 95

You can easily change the way Windows 95 looks and acts. You can change the colors displayed on the screen or adjust the date and time set in the computer.

Document Names

You can use up to 255 characters, including spaces, to name a document in Windows 95. This lets you give your documents descriptive names so they are easy to identify.

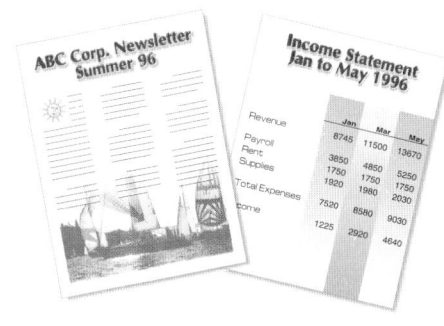

Plug and Play

Windows 95 supports the Plug and Play technology. This technology lets you add new features to a computer without complex and time-consuming installation procedures.

Windows Explorer

Like a map, Windows Explorer shows you the location of each folder and document on a computer. You can use Windows Explorer to move, open, print or delete documents.

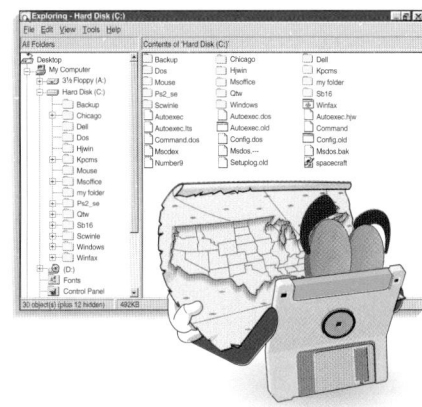

WINDOWS 95 FEATURES (CONTINUED)

WordPad and Paint

Windows 95 comes with a word processing program, called WordPad, that lets you create simple documents such as letters and memos. Windows 95 also includes a drawing program, called Paint, that lets you create pictures.

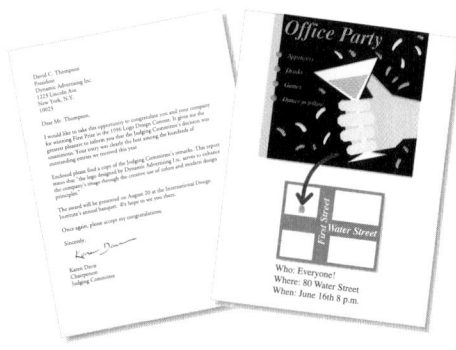

Computer Performance

Windows 95 comes with several features that will improve the performance of a computer. For example, the ScanDisk feature finds and repairs hard disk errors.

Backup

The Backup feature lets you copy important information stored on a computer to floppy disks or tape cartridges. This helps protect the information in case the original files are stolen or damaged due to viruses or computer failure.

Briefcase

The Briefcase feature lets you easily transfer files between your office and portable computers. This feature is useful if you work at home or while traveling. When you return to the office, Briefcase will update any documents you changed.

EXCHANGE INFORMATION

Microsoft Exchange

Windows 95 comes with Microsoft Exchange. This feature lets you exchange electronic mail with other people on a network or the Internet. You can also use this feature to send faxes to other computers or fax machines.

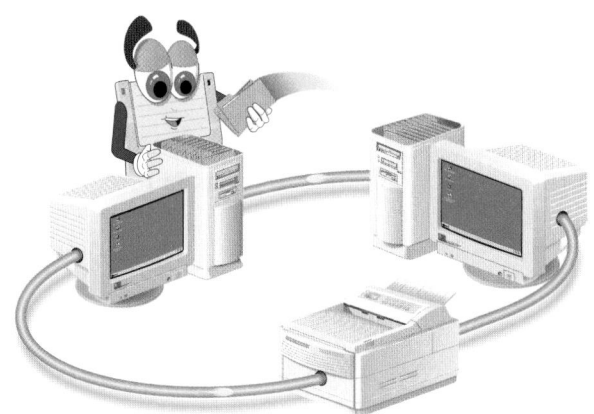

Networking

Windows 95 comes with features that let you share information and printers on a network. The Network Neighborhood feature lets you browse through and access information on all computers on a network. When at home or traveling, you can use the Dial-Up Networking feature to access information on the network at work.

WINDOWS NT

Windows NT is a powerful operating system that provides excellent security features. Like Windows 95, Windows NT is a true operating system and can use up to 255 characters to name documents. Windows NT was designed for users with powerful computer systems.

MACINTOSH COMPUTERS

WHAT IS A MAC?

Macintosh computers, or Macs, were introduced by Apple Computer in 1984. Macs were the first well-known commercial computers with a mouse, on-screen windows, menus and icons.

Mac-compatible computers, or clones, are available from companies such as Power Computing and Motorola. Mac-compatibles are usually faster and less expensive than Macs produced by Apple, but replacing parts can be inconvenient.

MAC VS. PC

Components

Macs almost always come equipped with components that you have to purchase separately for a PC.

Programs

There are fewer programs designed for Macs than for PCs. This is because Macs have a smaller share of the computer market. There are special cards or programs you can buy that let you run PC software on a Mac.

MAC PROGRAMS

PC PROGRAMS

MAC ADVANTAGES

Easy to Use

The graphical interface of a Mac makes this type of computer very easy to use.

Expandable

It is very easy to add new devices to a Mac. You can install most devices, such as an external hard drive, without opening up the computer.

Networking

A network is a group of connected computers that allow people to share information and equipment. Every Mac comes with built-in networking hardware. This makes it easy and inexpensive to connect Macs to a network.

Desktop Publishing

The fast display of images on screen and true WYSIWYG (What You See Is What You Get) have helped to establish Macs as the standard in the desktop publishing industry. Desktop publishing lets you create professional documents by integrating text and graphics on a page.

COMPUTER CASE

A computer case contains all the major components of a Mac computer system.

Desktop Case

A desktop case usually sits on a desk, under a monitor.

Tower Case

A tower case usually sits on the floor. This provides more desk space, but can be less convenient for inserting and removing floppy disks and CD-ROM discs.

ALL-IN-ONE CASE

An all-in-one case contains a monitor, disk drive, CD-ROM drive and speakers in a single unit.

PORTABLE

A portable is a small, lightweight computer that you can easily transport. A portable has a built-in keyboard and screen.

PORT

A port is a connector at the back of a computer where you plug in an external device.

Serial Ports

Serial ports connect a printer or modem.

Monitor Port

A monitor port connects a monitor.

SCSI Port

A Small Computer System Interface (SCSI) port allows you to attach up to seven separate devices to your computer. SCSI connections are very fast, which makes them ideal for connecting high-speed devices such as external hard drives, CD-ROM drives and scanners.

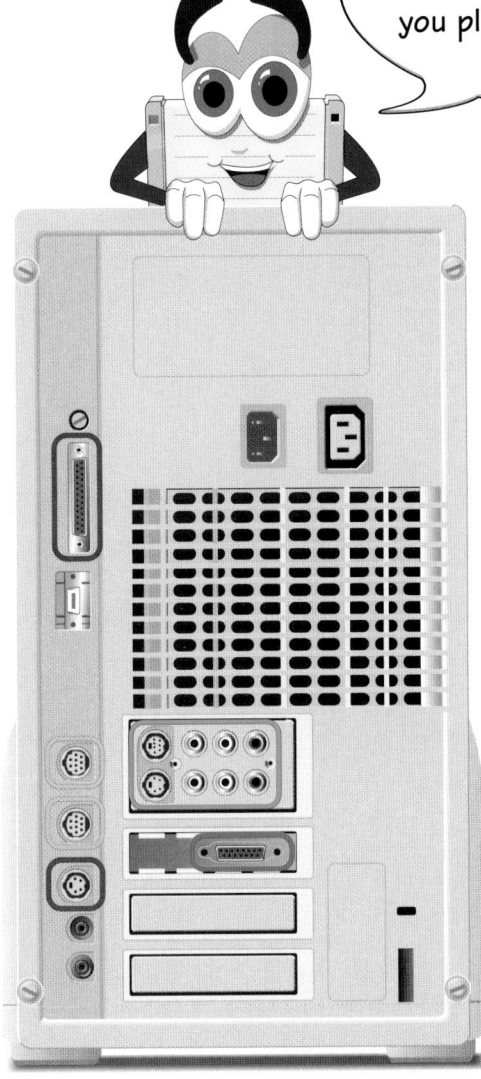

External Hard Drive

ADB Port

An Apple Desktop Bus (ADB) port connects a keyboard or mouse.

Audio/Video Port

High-end Macs have an Audio/Video port that connects a tape deck or Video Cassette Recorder (VCR). Low-end Macs only have a microphone port and a speaker port.

INPUT AND OUTPUT DEVICES

MOUSE

A mouse is a hand-held pointing device that lets you select and move items on your screen. Unlike a PC mouse, which has two buttons, a Mac mouse has only one button.

KEYBOARD

The keys on a keyboard let you enter information and instructions into a computer. The Mac keyboard has a **Command**, or **Apple**, key ( ) that you can use to quickly perform specific tasks. For example, in a word processing document, you can quickly make text bold by pressing and **B**.

PRINTER

A printer produces a paper copy of the information displayed on the screen. When buying a printer for a Mac, make sure the printer is Mac-compatible. A printer designed for a PC will not necessarily work with a Mac.

MONITOR

A monitor displays text and images generated by a computer. Some monitors are designed to work only with Macs. For more flexibility, you can buy a monitor that will work with both Macs and PCs.

VIDEO CARD

A video card translates instructions from the computer into a form the monitor can understand. Most Macs come with a built-in video card.

SOUND CHIP

A sound chip lets a computer play and record high-quality sound. All Macs come with a built-in sound chip.

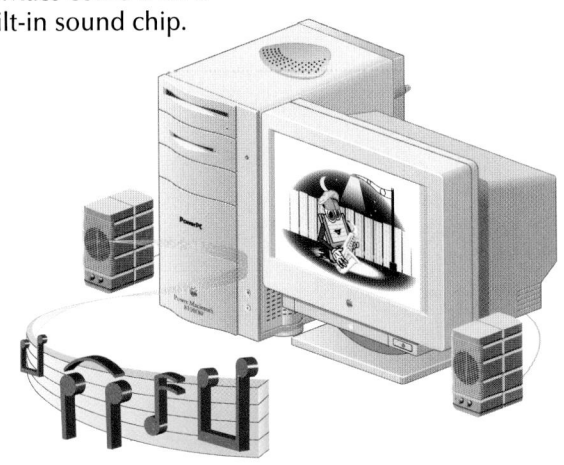

MODEM

A modem lets computers exchange information through telephone lines. Most Mac modems are external modems. An external modem sits outside a computer and plugs into the back of a computer.

CPU

The CPU processes instructions, performs calculations and manages the flow of information through a computer system.

> The Central Processing Unit (CPU) is the main chip in a computer.

CISC

Older Macs use Complex Instruction Set Computing (CISC) chips, such as the 68040 chip. CISC chips are slower than PowerPC chips and are now obsolete for the Mac.

PowerPC

Newer Macs use the much faster PowerPC chips, also called Reduced Instruction Set Computer (RISC) chips. PowerPC chips include 601, 603 and 604 chips.

Native Software

Native software is software designed especially for PowerPC chips. If you buy a computer with a PowerPC chip, make sure you buy native software to use on the computer. Native software runs much faster on a PowerPC computer than non-native software.

CPU GENERATIONS

Every CPU generation is available in several speeds. The speed of a CPU is measured in megahertz (MHz), or millions of cycles per second.

Each new generation of CPUs is more powerful than the one before.

68040

The 68040 chip is used in older Macs and can have speeds up to 40 MHz.

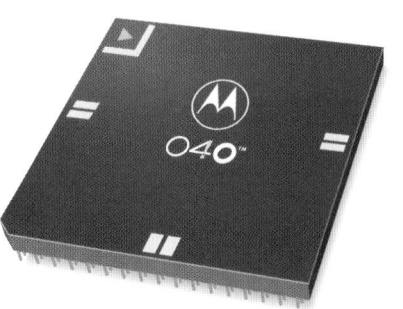

601

The 601 chip is the first generation of PowerPC chips and can have speeds up to 120 MHz.

603

The 603 chip is used in portable Macs as well as full-sized Macs and can have speeds up to 117 MHz. The faster 603e chip can have speeds up to 200 MHz.

604

604 chips can have speeds up to 150 MHz. The faster 604e chip is the most powerful PowerPC chip currently available for the Mac and can have speeds up to 225 MHz.

BUS

The efficiency of a bus depends on the bus width and the bus speed. Bus width is measured in bits. Bus speed is measured in megahertz (MHz), or millions of cycles per second.

NUBUS

The NuBus is found in all Macs with a 68040 CPU and in some Macs with a 601 or 603 CPU. The NuBus is a slower bus than the PCI bus.

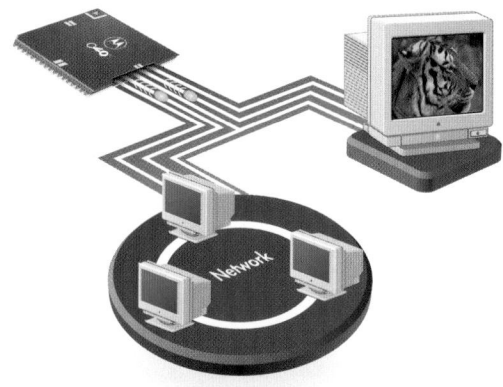

PCI BUS

The Peripheral Component Interconnect (PCI) bus is found in all Macs with a 604 CPU and in some Macs with a 601 or 603 CPU. The PCI bus offers better performance than the NuBus, especially when carrying large amounts of information, such as video files. Also, components designed for the PCI bus are less expensive than components designed for the NuBus.

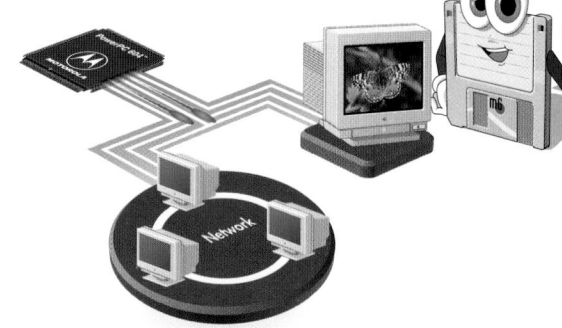

MEMORY

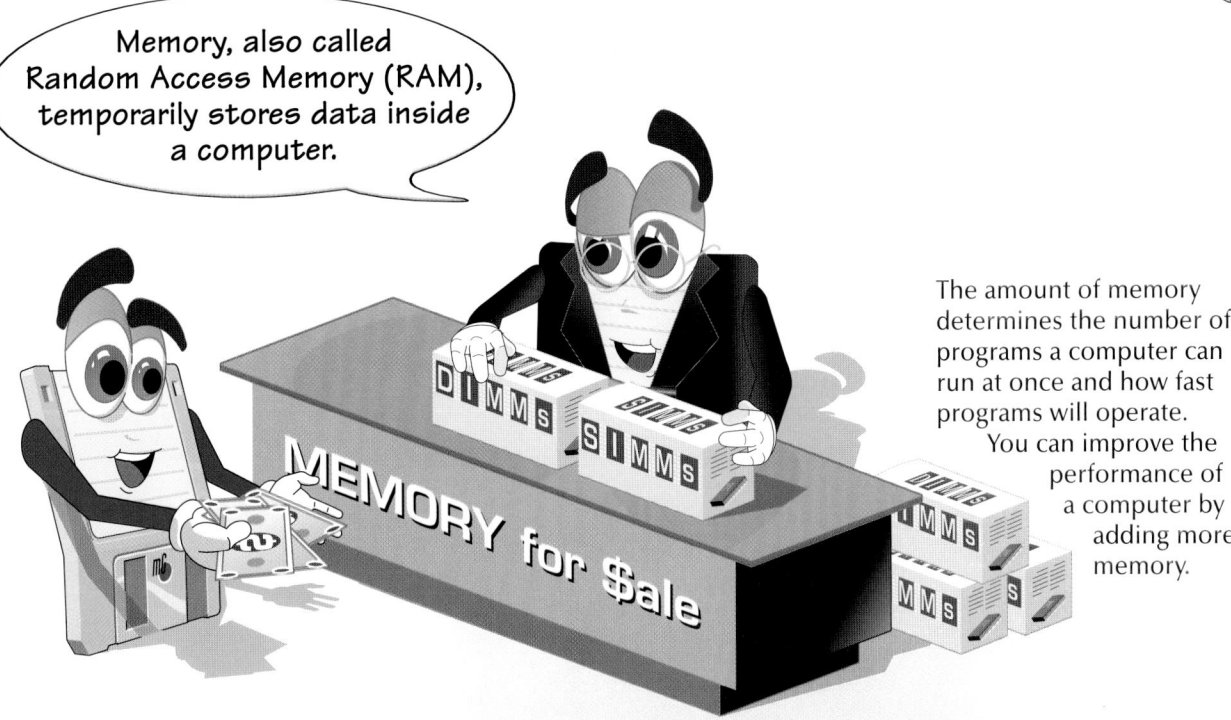

Memory, also called Random Access Memory (RAM), temporarily stores data inside a computer.

The amount of memory determines the number of programs a computer can run at once and how fast programs will operate. You can improve the performance of a computer by adding more memory.

CAPACITY

Memory is measured in bytes. You should buy a Mac with at least 16 MB of memory, but 32 MB of memory is recommended.

SIMM

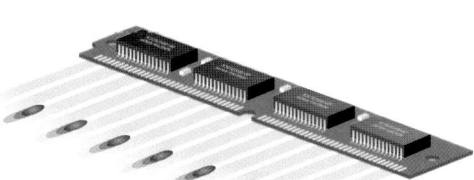

In all Macs with a 68040 or 603 CPU and in some Macs with a 601 CPU, memory is stored in Single In-line Memory Modules (SIMMs).

DIMM

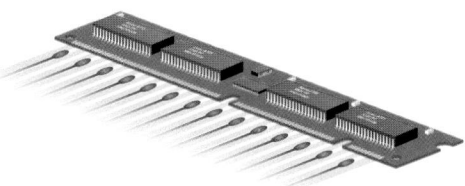

In some Macs with a 601 CPU and in all Macs with a 604 CPU, memory is stored in Dual In-line Memory Modules (DIMMs).

HARD DRIVE

The hard drive is the primary device that a computer uses to store information.

CAPACITY

The amount of information a hard drive can store is measured in bytes. A hard drive with a capacity of 1 GB will suit most home and business users.

Purchase the largest hard drive you can afford. New programs and data will quickly fill a hard drive.

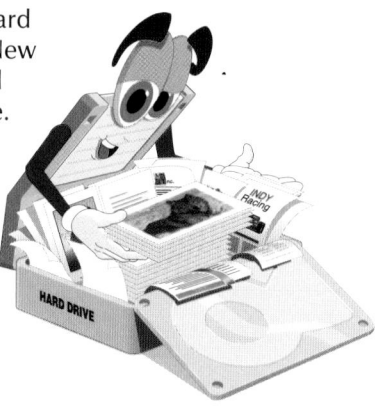

REMOVABLE HARD DRIVE

A removable hard drive lets you easily back up information on your hard drive or move large amounts of information from one computer to another. Popular removable hard drives for the Mac include SyQuest's SQ200 drive and Iomega's Zip drive.

FLOPPY DRIVE

A floppy drive stores and retrieves information on floppy disks.

A floppy disk is a removable device that magnetically stores data.

INSERT A FLOPPY DISK

Push the floppy disk gently into the drive, label side up. Most drives make a "click" sound when you have fully inserted the disk.

There is no eject button on a Mac floppy drive. You eject a disk by selecting **Eject Disk** from the Special menu on the computer screen.

PC FLOPPY DISKS

Newer Macs can use PC floppy disks as well as Mac floppy disks. You often need special software to translate the information on a PC floppy disk into a form you can use on a Mac.

OPERATING SYSTEMS

An operating system is the software that controls the overall activity of a computer.

System 6

System 6 is widely used in older, slower Macs because it does not require much memory to run.

System 7

Newer Macs use the more powerful System 7 operating system. System 7.5.3 is the most recent release of System 7. System 7.5.3 requires at least 8 MB of memory to run, but 16 MB of memory is recommended.

System 8

System 8 will soon be available. System 8 will have many new features, including preemptive multitasking. Preemptive multitasking means that if one program crashes, the whole computer system is not affected because each open program uses its own protected memory.

THE SYSTEM 7.5 SCREEN

Apple Menu

The Apple menu lets you quickly access certain applications, such as Calculator and Note Pad.

Menu Bar

Each menu in the menu bar lets you select various commands.

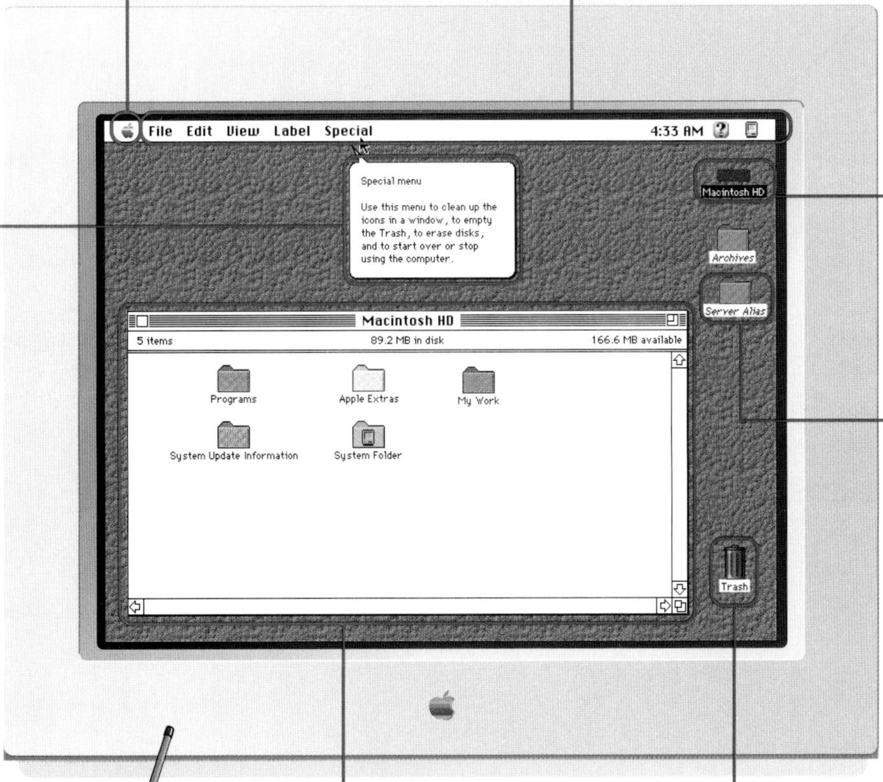

Balloon Help

Balloon Help is a Mac tool that can tell you about the items on your screen.

🍎 File Edit View Label Special   4:33 AM ❓ ▯

Special menu

Use this menu to clean up the icons in a window, to empty the Trash, to erase disks, and to start over or stop using the computer.

Macintosh HD

Archives

Server Alias

Macintosh HD

5 items   89.2 MB in disk   166.6 MB available

Programs   Apple Extras   My Work

System Update Information   System Folder

Trash

Hard Drive Icon

You can double-click the mouse on this icon to see the contents of your hard drive.

Alias

An alias provides a quick way to open a document or program you use regularly.

Window

A window is a rectangle that displays information on the screen. Each window has a title bar that displays the name of the window (example: Macintosh HD).

Trash

You can discard a file you no longer need by placing it in the Trash.

NETWORKS

INTRODUCTION TO NETWORKS

A network is a group of connected computers that allow people to share information and equipment.

TYPES OF NETWORKS

Local Area Network

A Local Area Network (LAN) is a network that connects computers within a small geographic area, such as a building.

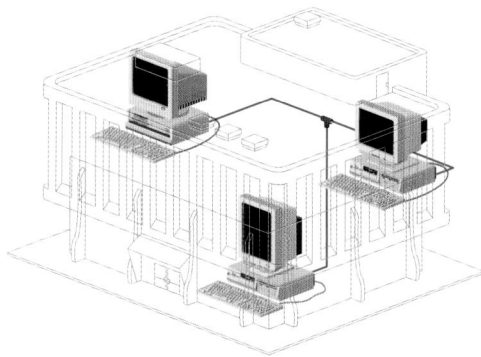

Wide Area Network

A Wide Area Network (WAN) is a network that connects computers across a large geographic area, such as a city or country. A WAN can transmit information by telephone line, microwave or satellite.

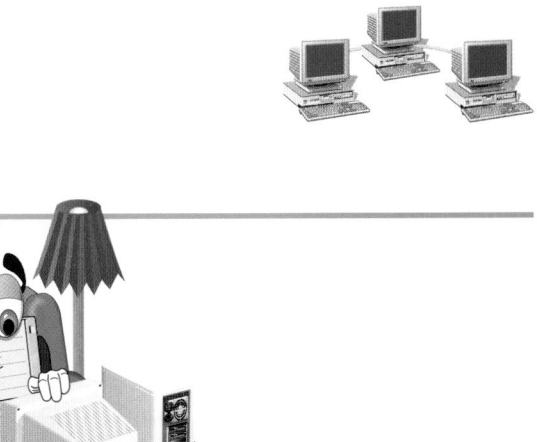

NETWORK ADVANTAGES

Work Away From Office

When traveling or at home, you can connect to the network at work to exchange messages and files.

Eliminate Sneakernet

Sneakernet refers to physically carrying information from one computer to another to exchange information. A computer network eliminates the need for sneakernet.

Share Information

Networks let you easily share data and programs. You can exchange documents, electronic mail, video, sound and images.

Share Equipment

Computers connected to a network can share equipment, such as a printer or modem.

NETWORK ADMINISTRATOR

A network administrator manages the network and makes sure the network runs smoothly. A network administrator may also be called a network manager, information systems manager or system administrator.

Electronic Mail

You can exchange electronic mail (e-mail) with other people on a network. Electronic mail saves paper and provides a fast and convenient way to exchange ideas and request information.

Groupware

Groupware is software that helps people on a network coordinate and manage projects. Groupware packages usually let you exchange electronic mail, schedule meetings, participate in online discussions and share corporate information. Popular groupware packages include Lotus Notes and Novell GroupWise.

Videoconferencing

Videoconferencing lets you have face-to-face conversations with other people on a network, whether they are around the corner or on the other side of the country. Using videoconferencing software and equipment, you can see and hear the people you are communicating with.

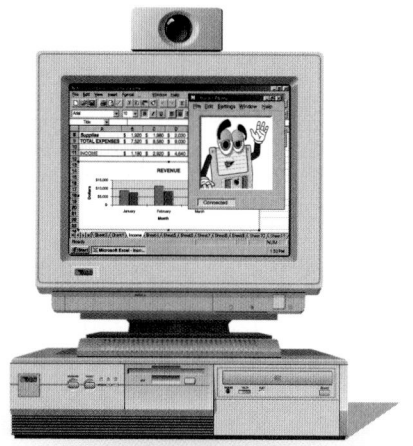

PARTS OF A NETWORK

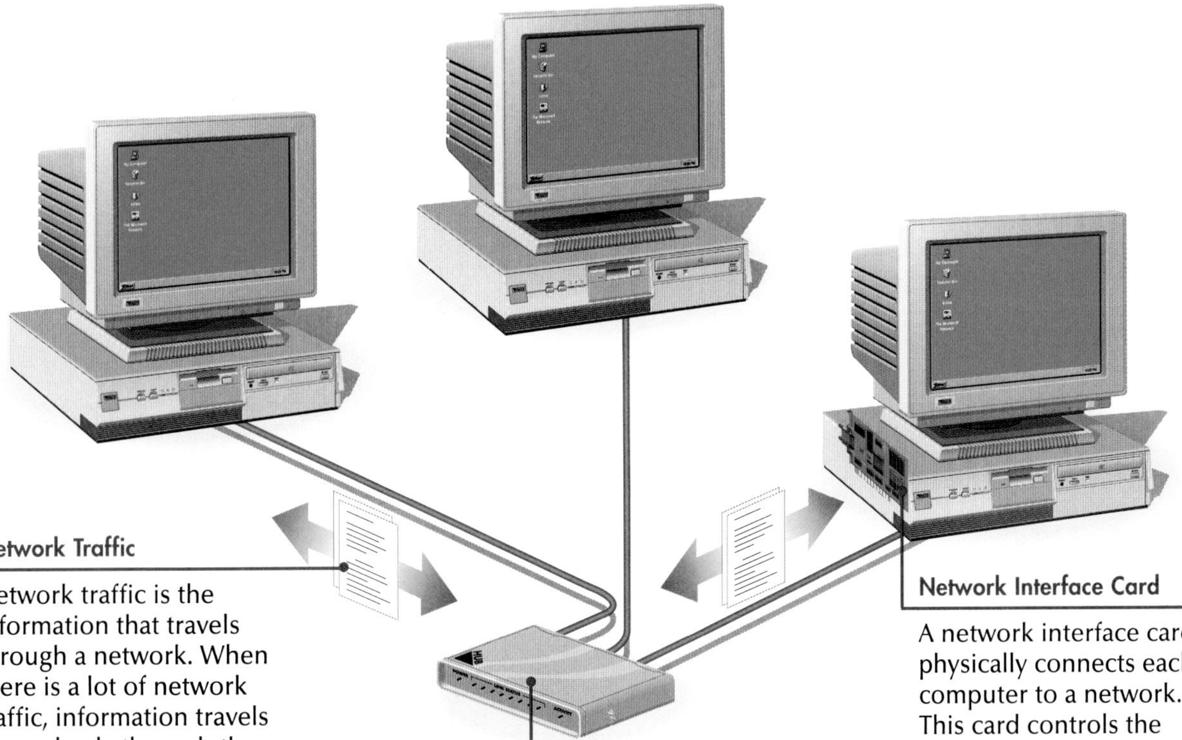

Network Traffic

Network traffic is the information that travels through a network. When there is a lot of network traffic, information travels more slowly through the network.

Hub

A hub provides a central location where all the cables on a network come together.

Network Interface Card

A network interface card physically connects each computer to a network. This card controls the flow of information between the network and the computer.

Cables

Cables connect computers and equipment to a network. There are four main types of cables—coaxial, Unshielded Twisted Pair (UTP), Shielded Twisted Pair (STP) and fiber optic. Fiber optic cable is the most expensive type of cable, but it can carry information faster and over longer distances.

HOW INFORMATION IS STORED

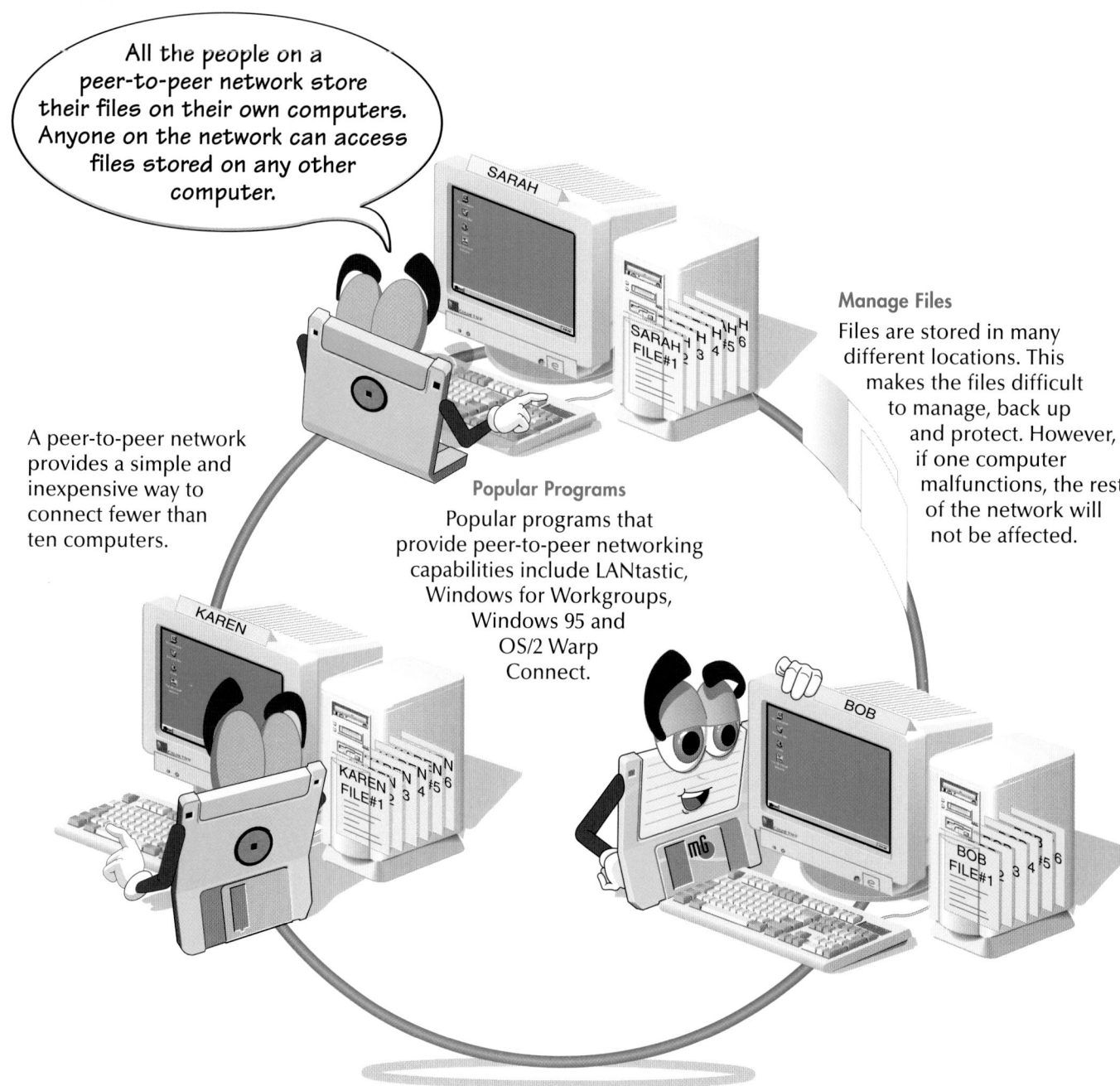

All the people on a peer-to-peer network store their files on their own computers. Anyone on the network can access files stored on any other computer.

A peer-to-peer network provides a simple and inexpensive way to connect fewer than ten computers.

Popular Programs

Popular programs that provide peer-to-peer networking capabilities include LANtastic, Windows for Workgroups, Windows 95 and OS/2 Warp Connect.

Manage Files

Files are stored in many different locations. This makes the files difficult to manage, back up and protect. However, if one computer malfunctions, the rest of the network will not be affected.

CLIENT/SERVER NETWORK

All the people on a client/server network store their files on a central computer. Everyone connected to the network can access the files stored on the central computer.

Server

The server is the central computer that stores the files of every person on the network.

Manage Files

All the files are stored on the server. This makes the files easy to manage, back up and protect. However, if the server malfunctions, the entire network will be affected.

A client/server network provides a highly efficient way to connect ten or more computers or computers exchanging large amounts of information.

Popular Programs

Popular programs that provide client/server networking capabilities include NetWare and Windows NT.

Client

A client is a computer that can access information stored on the server.

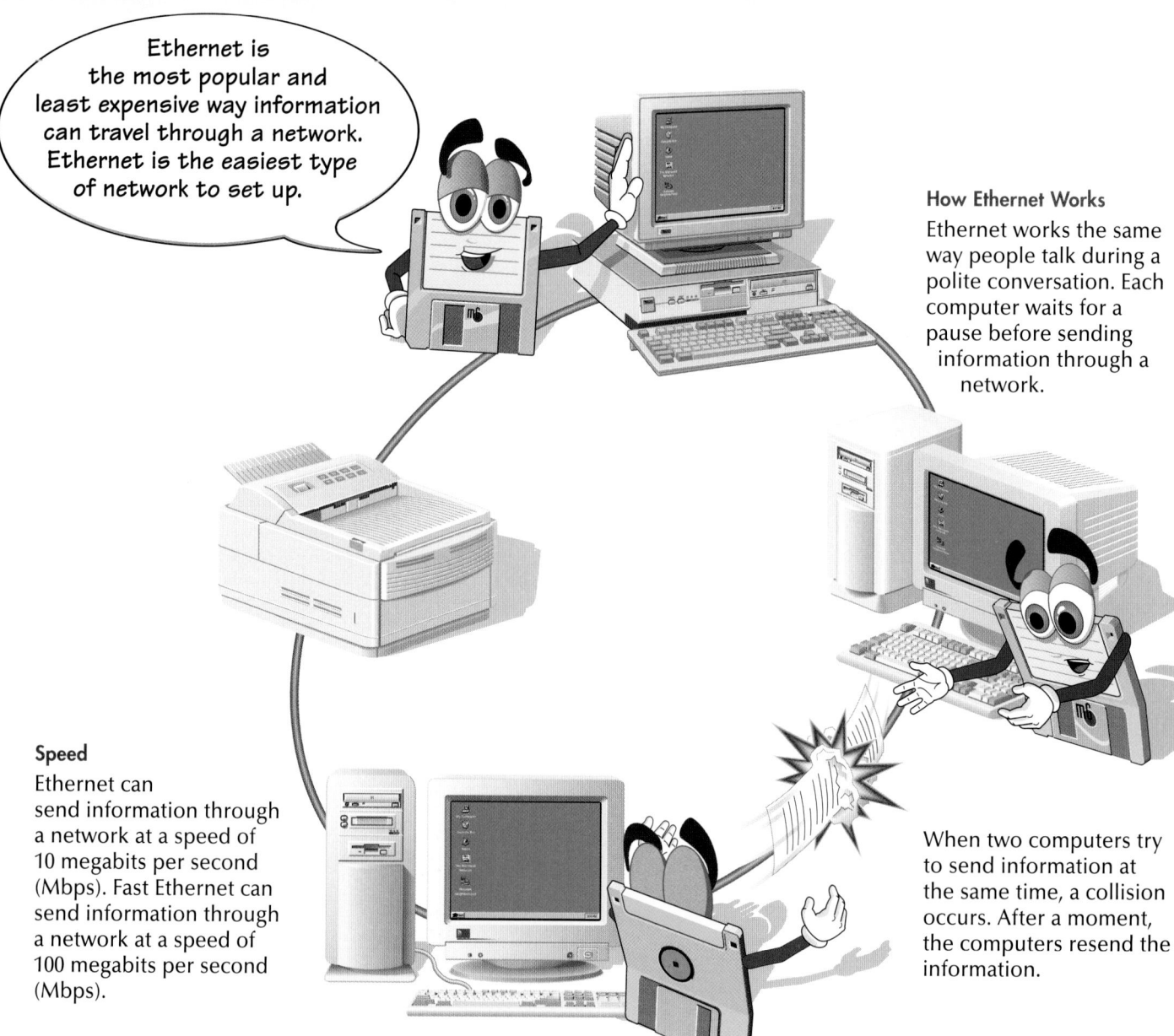

Ethernet is the most popular and least expensive way information can travel through a network. Ethernet is the easiest type of network to set up.

How Ethernet Works

Ethernet works the same way people talk during a polite conversation. Each computer waits for a pause before sending information through a network.

Speed

Ethernet can send information through a network at a speed of 10 megabits per second (Mbps). Fast Ethernet can send information through a network at a speed of 100 megabits per second (Mbps).

When two computers try to send information at the same time, a collision occurs. After a moment, the computers resend the information.

TOKEN-RING

Token-ring is a type of network often found in large organizations, such as banks and insurance companies.

How Token-Ring Works

Token-ring works by passing a single token from computer to computer. The token collects and delivers information as it travels around the network.

Speed

A token-ring network can send information through a network at speeds of 4 or 16 megabits per second (Mbps).

ATM

Asynchronous Transfer Mode (ATM) is a faster, more powerful way to exchange information on a network.

How ATM Works

ATM works by sending information through a network in equal-sized pieces, called cells.

Speed

ATM can send information through a network at speeds of 25, 155 or 622 megabits per second (Mbps).

NETWORK SECURITY

FIREWALL

A firewall is special software or hardware designed to protect a private computer network from unauthorized access. Firewalls are used by corporations, banks and research facilities to keep information private and secure.

USER NAME AND PASSWORD

You usually have to enter a user name and password when you want to access information on a network. This ensures that only authorized people can use the information stored on the network.

Choose a Password

When choosing a password, do not use words that people can easily associate with you, such as your name or favorite sport. The most effective password connects two words or number sequences with a special character (example: easy@123). To increase security, memorize your password and do not write it down.

jim#96
happy#44

INTRANET

An intranet is a small version of the Internet inside an office.

ABC COMPANY

Information

An intranet is a very efficient and inexpensive way to make internal company documents available to employees. Companies use intranets to distribute information such as phone directories, product listings and job openings.

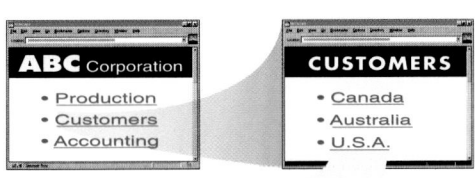

ABC Corporation
- Production
- Customers
- Accounting

CUSTOMERS
- Canada
- Australia
- U.S.A.

U.S.A. Customers
- Sunset Inc., 258 Linton Ave., New York, NY 10010
- Booklovers Inc., 50 Tree Lane, Boston, MA 02117
- EGA Inc., 47 Cosby Ave., Las Vegas, NV 89116
- Bobs Electronics, 10 Heldon St., Atlanta, GA 30367
- Hans Cookies, 890 Bun St., San Diego, CA 92121

Connected Documents

Documents on an intranet are connected. Employees can select highlighted text in one document to display another, related document.

Programs

The program you use to browse through information on an intranet is the same program you would use to browse through information on the World Wide Web.

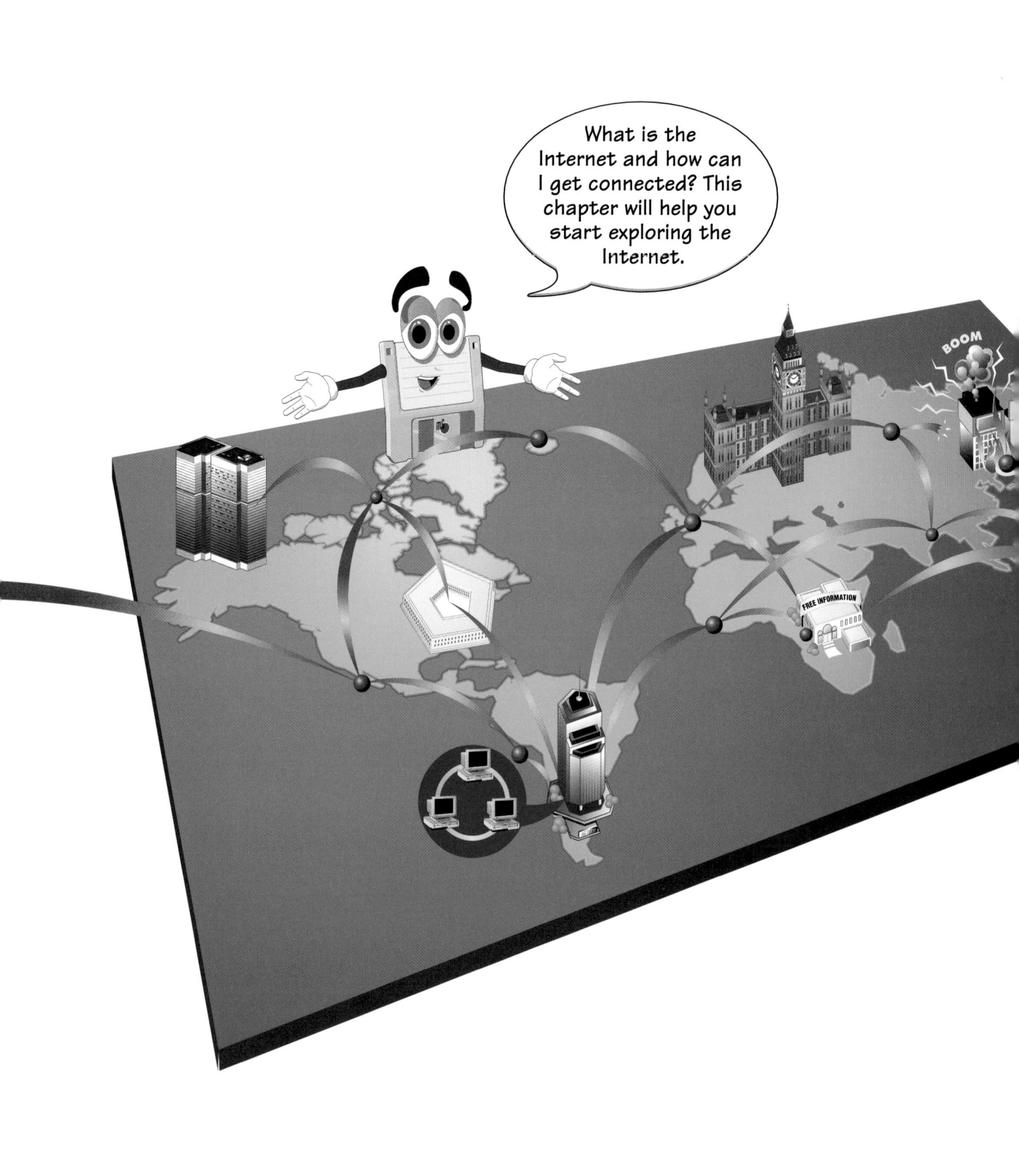

THE INTERNET

INTRODUCTION TO THE INTERNET

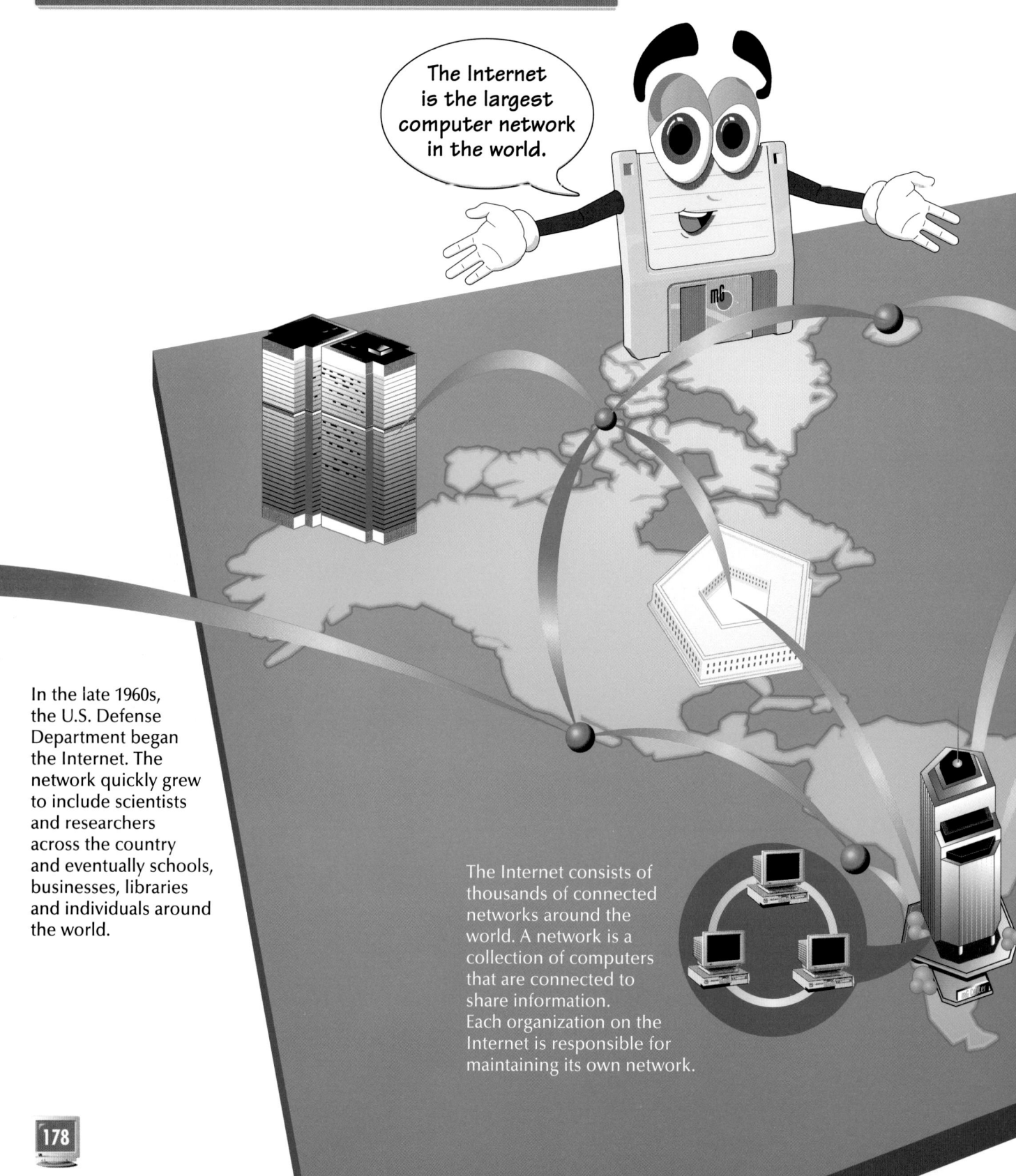

The Internet is the largest computer network in the world.

In the late 1960s, the U.S. Defense Department began the Internet. The network quickly grew to include scientists and researchers across the country and eventually schools, businesses, libraries and individuals around the world.

The Internet consists of thousands of connected networks around the world. A network is a collection of computers that are connected to share information. Each organization on the Internet is responsible for maintaining its own network.

If part of the Internet fails,
information finds a
new route around the
disabled computers.

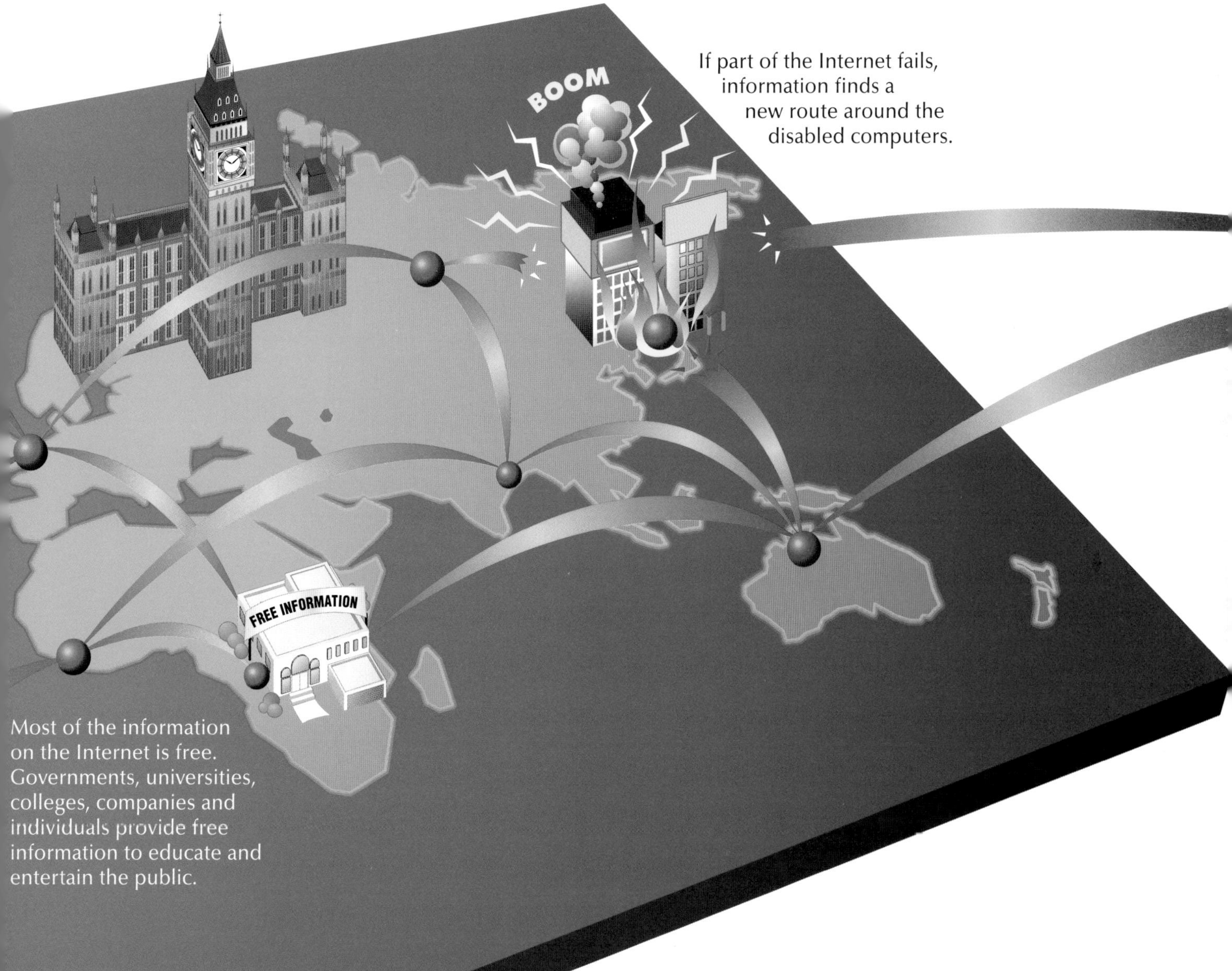

Most of the information
on the Internet is free.
Governments, universities,
colleges, companies and
individuals provide free
information to educate and
entertain the public.

The Internet is
often called
the Net, the
Information
Superhighway
or Cyber-space.

WHAT THE INTERNET OFFERS

ELECTRONIC MAIL

Exchanging electronic mail (e-mail) is the most popular feature on the Internet. You can exchange electronic mail with people around the world, including friends, colleagues, family members, customers and even people you meet on the Internet. Electronic mail is fast, easy, inexpensive and saves paper.

INFORMATION

The Internet gives you access to information on any subject imaginable. You can review newspapers, magazines, academic papers, government documents, television show transcripts, famous speeches, recipes, job listings, works by Shakespeare, airline schedules and much more.

Governments, colleges, universities, companies and individuals all offer free information on the Internet.

PROGRAMS

Thousands of programs are available on the Internet. These programs include word processors, spreadsheets, games and much more.

ENTERTAINMENT

Hundreds of simple games are available for free on the Internet, including backgammon, chess, poker, football and much more.

The Internet also lets you review current movies, hear television theme songs, read movie scripts and have interactive conversations with people around the world—even celebrities.

DISCUSSION GROUPS

You can join discussion groups on the Internet to meet people around the world with similar interests. You can ask questions, discuss problems and read interesting stories.

There are thousands of discussion groups on topics such as the environment, food, humor, music, pets, photography, politics, religion, sports and television.

ONLINE SHOPPING

You can order goods and services on the Internet without ever leaving your desk. You can buy items such as books, computer programs, flowers, music CDs, pizza, stocks, used cars and much more.

HOW INFORMATION TRANSFERS

All computers on the Internet work together to transfer information around the world.

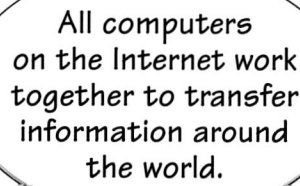

Packets

When you send information over the Internet, the information is broken down into smaller pieces, called packets. Each packet travels independently over the Internet and may take a different path to arrive at the intended destination.

When information arrives at its destination, the packets are reassembled.

TCP/IP

Transmission Control Protocol/Internet Protocol (TCP/IP) is a language computers on the Internet use to communicate with each other. TCP/IP divides information you send into packets and sends the packets over the Internet. When information arrives at the intended destination, TCP/IP ensures that all the packets arrived safely.

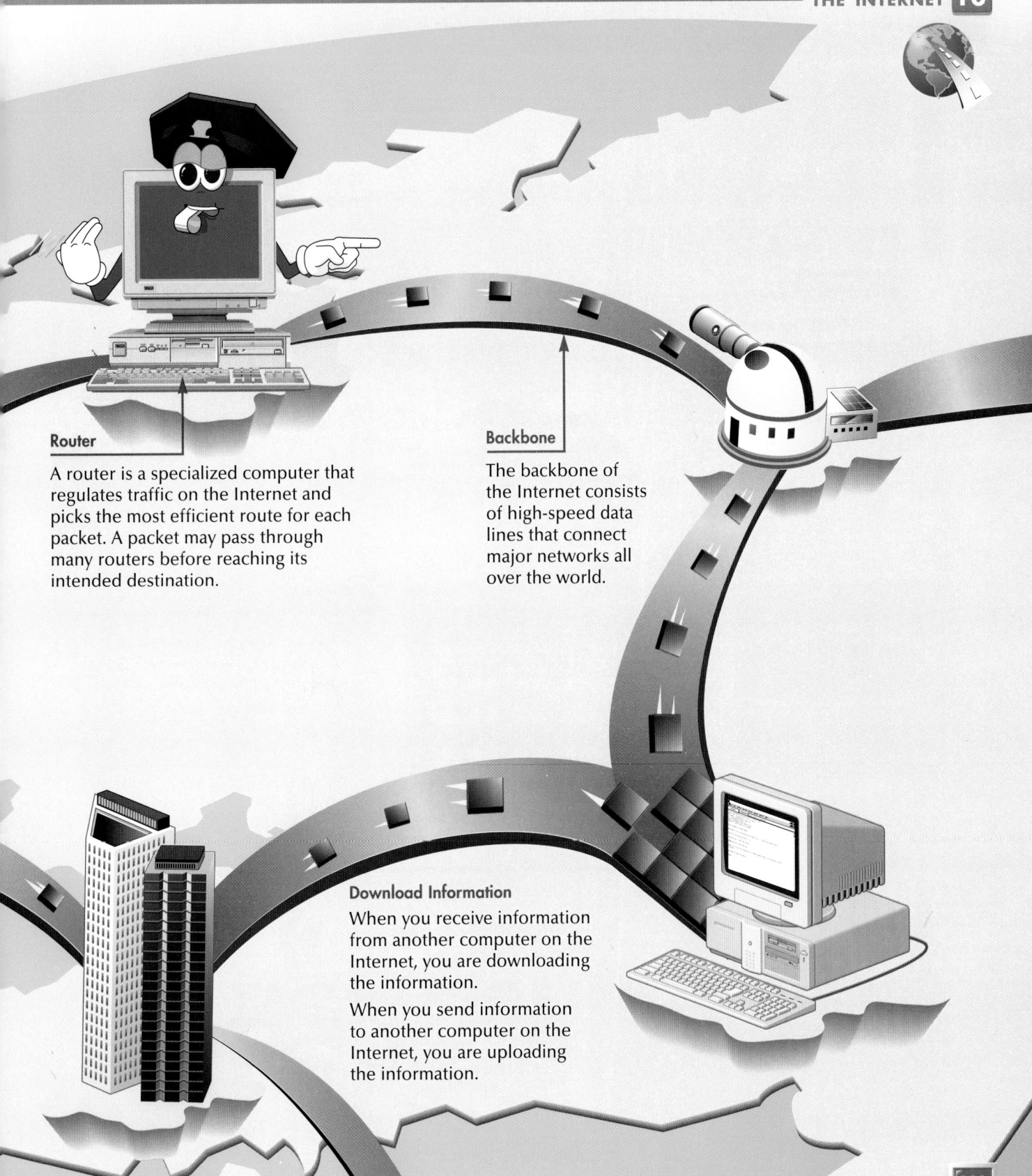

Router

A router is a specialized computer that regulates traffic on the Internet and picks the most efficient route for each packet. A packet may pass through many routers before reaching its intended destination.

Backbone

The backbone of the Internet consists of high-speed data lines that connect major networks all over the world.

Download Information

When you receive information from another computer on the Internet, you are downloading the information.

When you send information to another computer on the Internet, you are uploading the information.

GETTING CONNECTED

You need specific equipment and programs to connect to the Internet.

COMPUTER

You can use any type of computer, such as an IBM-compatible or Macintosh computer, to connect to the Internet.

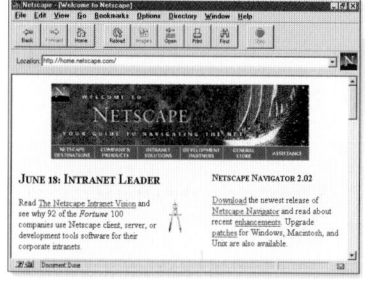

PROGRAMS

You need special programs to use the Internet. Most companies that connect you to the Internet provide the programs you need free of charge.

MODEM

You need a modem to connect to the Internet. Choose a modem with a speed of at least 14,400 bps, although a modem with a speed of 28,800 bps is recommended. For more information on modems, refer to page 44.

INTERNET SERVICE PROVIDER

An Internet Service Provider (ISP) is a company that gives you access to the Internet for a fee.

Cost

Many providers offer you a certain number of hours per day or month for a set fee. If you exceed the total number of hours, you are usually charged for every extra hour you use the provider.

Some providers offer unlimited access to the Internet for a set fee. Make sure you are aware of any hidden charges or restrictions.

COMMERCIAL ONLINE SERVICE

A commercial online service is a company that offers a vast amount of information and access to the Internet for a fee.

Popular online services include America Online, CompuServe and The Microsoft Network.

Cost

Most commercial online services let you try their service free of charge for a limited time. After the trial period, most online services offer a certain number of hours per day or month for a set fee.

If you exceed the total number of hours, you are usually charged for every extra hour you use the online service.

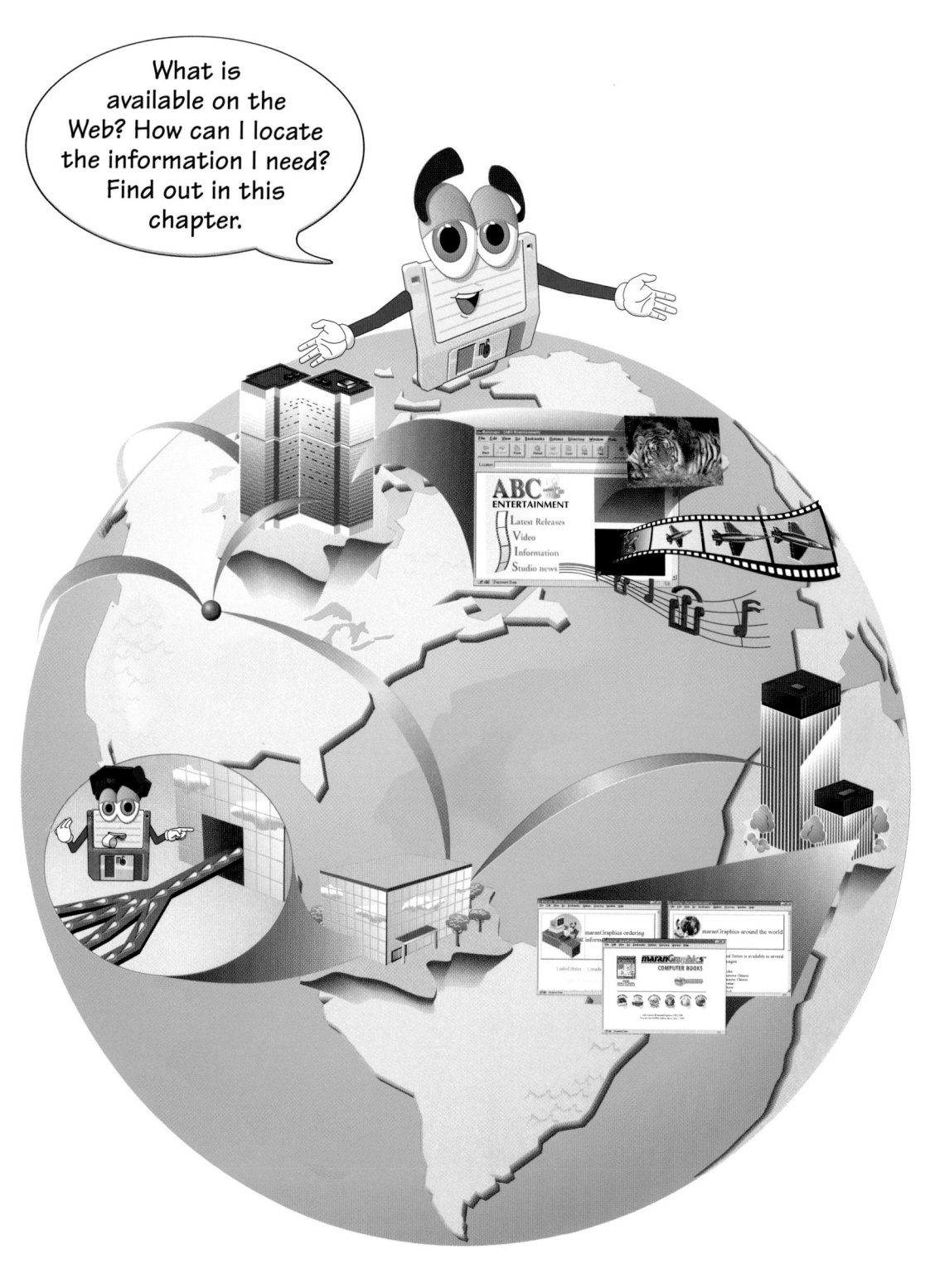

THE WORLD WIDE WEB

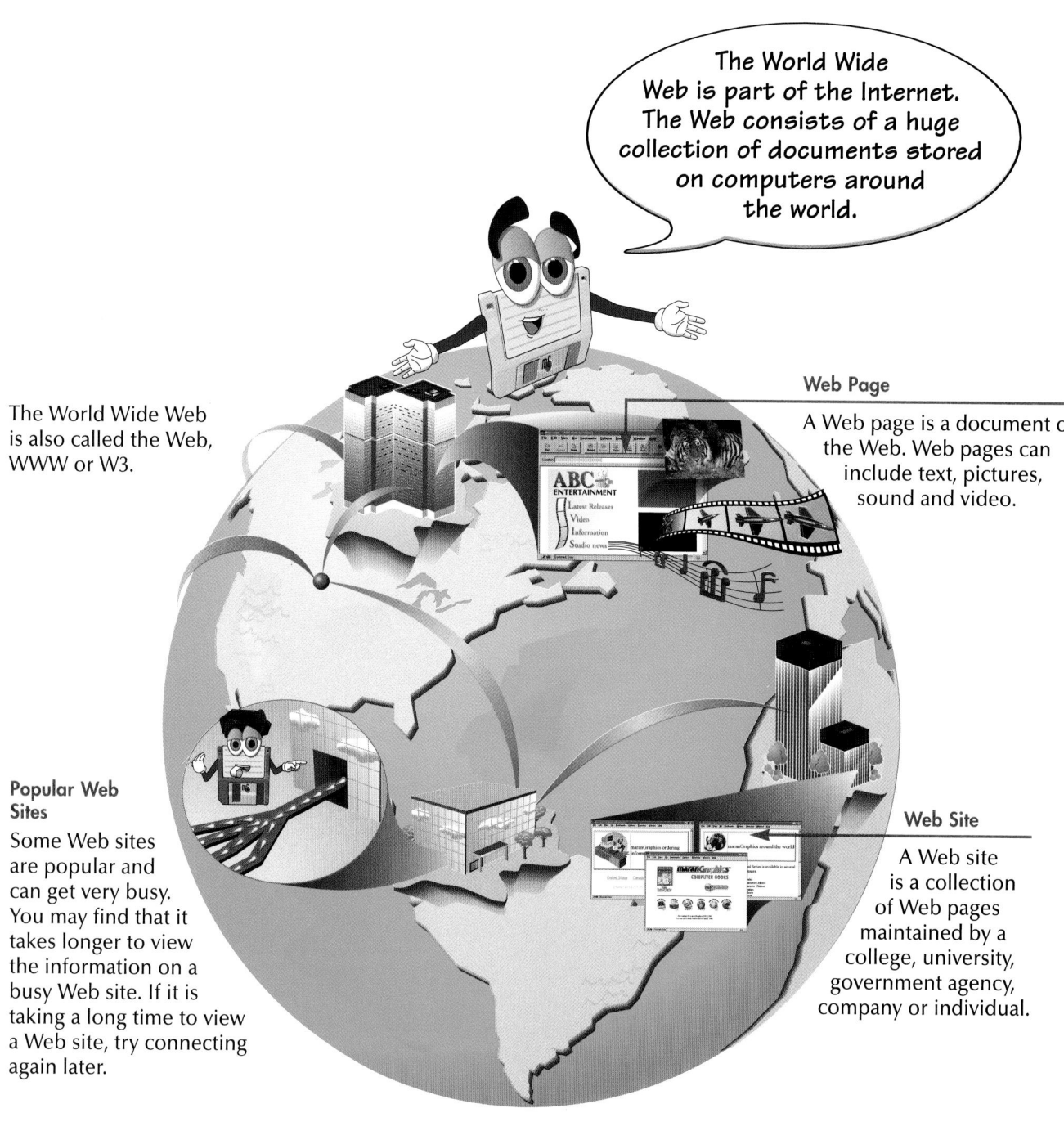

The World Wide Web is part of the Internet. The Web consists of a huge collection of documents stored on computers around the world.

The World Wide Web is also called the Web, WWW or W3.

Web Page

A Web page is a document on the Web. Web pages can include text, pictures, sound and video.

Popular Web Sites

Some Web sites are popular and can get very busy. You may find that it takes longer to view the information on a busy Web site. If it is taking a long time to view a Web site, try connecting again later.

Web Site

A Web site is a collection of Web pages maintained by a college, university, government agency, company or individual.

URL

Each Web page has a unique address, called the Uniform Resource Locator (URL). You can instantly display any Web page if you know its URL.

http://www.maran.com

■ All Web page URLs start with http (HyperText Transfer Protocol).

HYPERTEXT

Web pages are hypertext documents. A hypertext document contains highlighted text that connects to other pages on the Web. You can easily jump from one Web page to another by selecting the highlighted text.

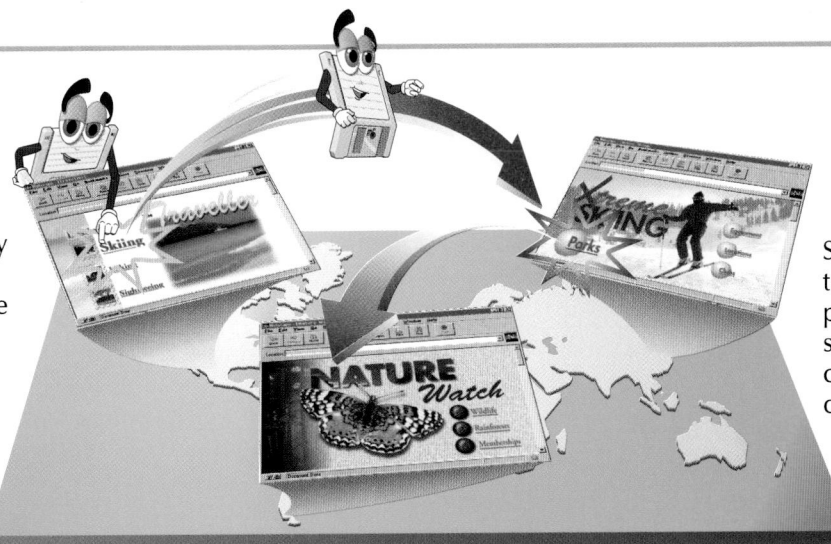

Selecting highlighted text can take you to a page located on the same computer or a computer across the city, country or world.

WEB BROWSER

A Web browser is a program that lets you view and explore information on the Web.

POPULAR BROWSERS

Netscape Navigator is currently the most popular browser. Other popular browsers include Microsoft Internet Explorer and NCSA Mosaic.

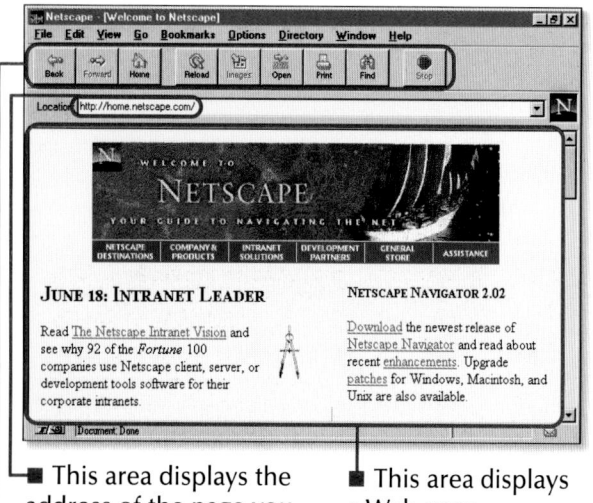

■ This area displays the address of the page you are currently viewing.

■ This area displays a toolbar to help you quickly perform common tasks.

■ This area displays a Web page.

HOME PAGE

The home page is the page that appears each time you start a Web browser.

You can choose any page on the Web as your home page. Make sure you choose a home page that provides a good starting point for exploring the Web.

Bookmarks

The bookmarks feature lets you store the addresses of Web pages you frequently visit. Bookmarks save you from having to remember and constantly retype your favorite Web page addresses. The bookmarks feature is also called a hotlist or favorites feature.

History

The History feature keeps track of all the pages you have viewed since you last started the Web browser. This feature lets you instantly return to any of the pages you have viewed.

Turn Off Graphics

Graphics, or pictures, may take a while to appear on the screen. You can save time by turning off the display of graphics. When you turn off the display of graphics, an icon (example: 🖼) will appear in place of any graphics.

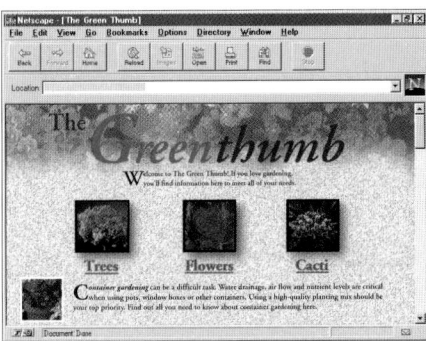

GRAPHICS ON

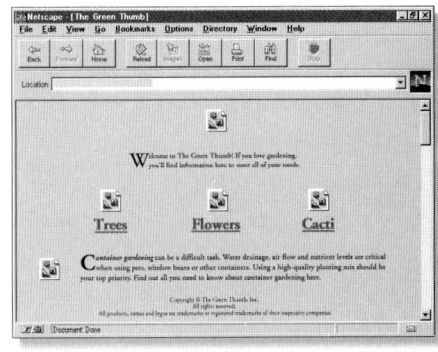

GRAPHICS OFF

MULTIMEDIA ON THE WEB

A Web page can contain text, graphics, sound, video and animation.

A Web browser needs special programs, called plug-ins or helpers, to work with certain types of files on the Web. These programs perform tasks that a browser cannot perform on its own. Most plug-ins and helpers are available for free on the Web.

Text

You can view documents on the Web such as newspapers, magazines, plays, famous speeches and television show transcripts.

Text transfers quickly to your computer, so you do not have to wait long to read text on a Web page.

Graphics

You can view graphics on the Web such as album covers, pictures of celebrities and famous paintings.

Sound

You can hear sound on the Web such as TV theme songs, movie soundtracks, sound effects and historical speeches.

Video and Animation

You can view video and animation on the Web such as movie clips, cartoons and interviews with celebrities.

3-D Worlds

You can view three-dimensional worlds and objects on the Web.

3-D worlds are created using a language called Virtual Reality Modeling Language (VRML).

You can use your mouse or keyboard to move through three-dimensional rooms or walk around a virtual object.

Java

Java is a programming language that allows Web pages to display animation and moving text, play music and much more.

You can find many examples of Java at: http://www.gamelan.com

SHOPPING ON THE WEB

You can buy products and services on the Web without ever leaving your desk.

SHOPPING MALLS

There are shopping malls on the Web where you can view and buy all kinds of products and services.

You can view a list of shopping malls on the Web at:

http://nsns.com/MouseTracks/HallofMalls.html

Many companies allow you to view and buy their products on the Web.

You can view a list of companies on the Web at:

http://www.bizweb.com

SECURITY

Security is very important when you want to send confidential information, such as credit card numbers or bank records, over the Internet.

You can safely transfer confidential information to a secure site on the Web. The address of a secure site usually starts with https rather than http.

SEARCH THE WEB

There are many free services you can use to find information on the Web. These services are called search tools.

A search tool catalogs Web pages to make them easier to find. Some search tools record every word on a Web page, while others only record the name of each page.

You can see a list of various search tools at the following Web sites:

http://www.search.com/alpha.html

http://home.netscape.com/home/internet-search.html

POPULAR SEARCH TOOLS

There are three popular search tools that can help you find information on the Web.

You can browse through categories, such as arts or sports, to find information that interests you or you can search for a specific word or topic.

AltaVista
http://www.altavista.digital.com

Infoseek
http://www.infoseek.com

Yahoo
http://www.yahoo.com

You can exchange electronic mail (e-mail) with people around the world.

E-mail provides a fast, economical and convenient way to send messages to family, friends and colleagues.

E-MAIL PROGRAM

An e-mail program lets you send, receive and manage your e-mail messages.

Popular e-mail programs include Netscape Mail and Eudora.

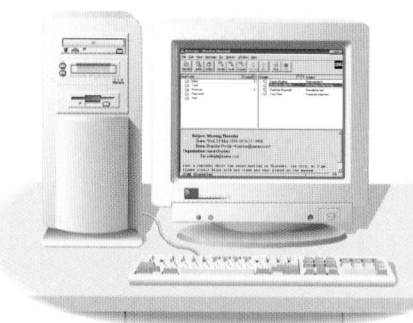

NETSCAPE MAIL

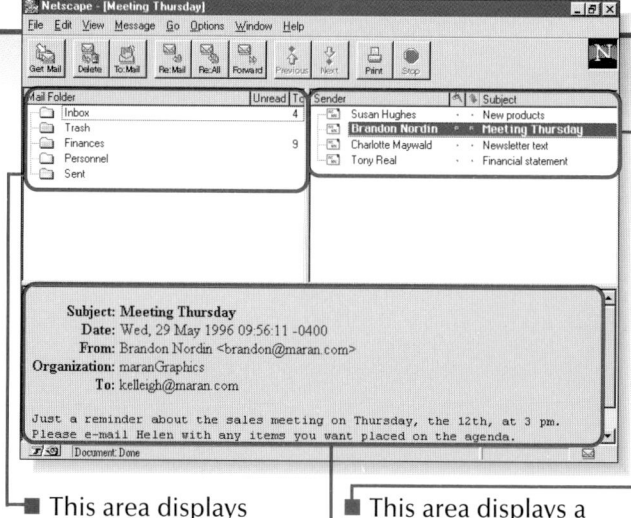

■ This area displays the folders that contain your e-mail messages.

■ This area displays a list of all your e-mail messages.

■ This area displays the contents of a single e-mail message.

E-MAIL ADDRESSES

> You can send a message to anyone around the world if you know the person's e-mail address.

mvickers@sales.abc.com

An e-mail address defines the location of an individual's mailbox on the Internet.

PARTS OF AN E-MAIL ADDRESS

An e-mail address consists of two parts separated by the @ ("at") symbol. An e-mail address cannot contain spaces.

mvickers@sales.abc.com

■ The user name is the name of the person's account. This can be a real name or a nickname.

■ The domain name is the location of the person's account on the Internet. Periods (.) separate the various parts of the domain name.

ORGANIZATION OR COUNTRY

The last few characters in an e-mail address usually indicate the type of organization or country to which the person belongs.

ORGANIZATION		COUNTRY	
com	commercial	au	Australia
edu	education	ca	Canada
gov	government	it	Italy
mil	military	jp	Japan
net	network	uk	United Kingdom
org	organization (often non-profit)	us	United States

CREATE A MESSAGE

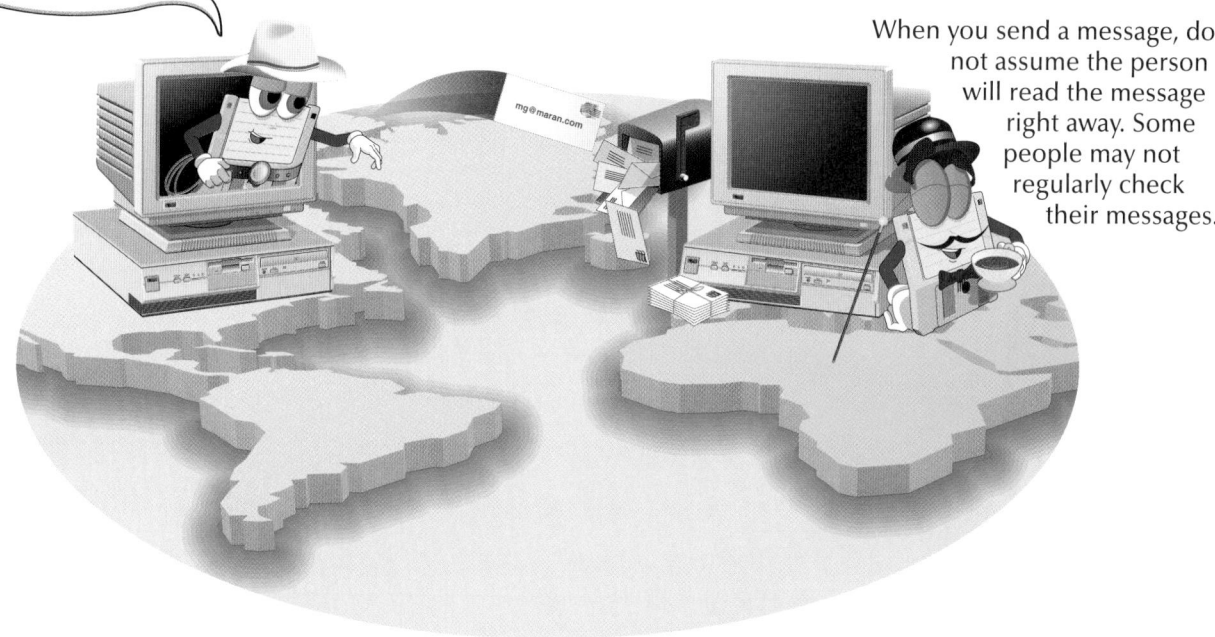

You can send a message to exchange ideas or request information.

When you send a message, do not assume the person will read the message right away. Some people may not regularly check their messages.

COST

Once you pay a service provider for a connection to the Internet, there is no charge for sending and receiving e-mail. You do not have to pay extra even if you send a long message or the message travels around the world.

Exchanging e-mail can save you money on long distance calls. The next time you are about to pick up the telephone, consider sending an e-mail message instead.

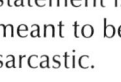

WRITING STYLE

Make sure every message you send is clear, concise and contains no spelling or grammar errors. Also make sure the message will not be misinterpreted. For example, the reader may not realize a statement is meant to be sarcastic.

MESSAGE TIPS

Smileys

You can use special characters, called smileys or emoticons, to express emotions in messages. These characters resemble human faces if you turn them sideways.

SMILEYS

Gesture	Characters
Cry	:'-(
Frown	:-(
Indifferent	:-I
Laugh	:-D
Smile	:-)
Surprise	:-O
Wink	;-)

Abbreviations

Abbreviations are commonly used in messages to save time typing.

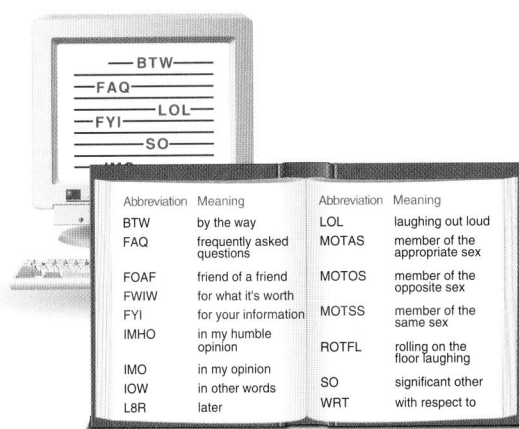

Abbreviation	Meaning	Abbreviation	Meaning
BTW	by the way	LOL	laughing out loud
FAQ	frequently asked questions	MOTAS	member of the appropriate sex
FOAF	friend of a friend	MOTOS	member of the opposite sex
FWIW	for what it's worth		
FYI	for your information	MOTSS	member of the same sex
IMHO	in my humble opinion	ROTFL	rolling on the floor laughing
IMO	in my opinion		
IOW	in other words	SO	significant other
L8R	later	WRT	with respect to

Shouting

A MESSAGE WRITTEN IN CAPITAL LETTERS IS ANNOYING AND HARD TO READ. THIS IS CALLED SHOUTING.

Always use upper and lower case letters when typing messages.

Flame

A flame is an angry or insulting message directed at one person. A flame war is an argument that continues for a while. Avoid starting or participating in flame wars.

E-MAIL FEATURES

RECEIVE A MESSAGE

You do not have to be at your computer to receive a message. Your service provider keeps all your messages until you retrieve them. Make sure you regularly check for messages.

You can use most computers with a modem to connect to your service provider and retrieve messages. This means you can retrieve your messages when traveling.

REPLY TO A MESSAGE

You can reply to a message to answer a question, express an opinion or supply additional information.

When you reply to a message, make sure you include part of the original message. This is called quoting. Quoting helps the reader identify which message you are replying to. To save the reader time, make sure you delete all parts of the original message that do not directly relate to your reply.

ATTACH A FILE TO A MESSAGE

You can attach a document, picture, sound, video or program to a message you are sending.

Many e-mail programs use Multipurpose Internet Mail Extensions (MIME) to attach files to messages.

To view an attached file, the computer receiving the message must be able to understand MIME. The computer must also have a program that can view or play the file.

FORWARD A MESSAGE

After reading a message, you can add comments and then send the message to a friend or colleague.

PRINT A MESSAGE

You can print a message to produce a paper copy of the message.

MAILING LISTS

A mailing list is a discussion group that uses e-mail to communicate.

When a mailing list receives a message, a copy of the message goes to everyone on the mailing list.

There are thousands of mailing lists that cover a wide variety of topics, from aromatherapy to Led Zeppelin. New mailing lists are created every week.

MANUALLY MAINTAINED LISTS

A person manages a manually maintained mailing list.

A manually maintained list usually contains the word "request" in its e-mail address (example: hang-gliding-request@lists.utah.edu).

AUTOMATED LISTS

A computer program manages an automated mailing list. There are three popular programs that manage automated lists—listproc, listserv and majordomo.

An automated list typically contains the name of the program that manages the list in its e-mail address (example: majordomo@teleport.com).

SUBSCRIBE TO A MAILING LIST

Just as you would subscribe to a newspaper or magazine, you can subscribe to a mailing list that interests you.

Subscribing adds your e-mail address to the mailing list.

Unsubscribe

If you no longer want to receive messages from a mailing list, you can unsubscribe from the mailing list at any time. Unsubscribing removes your e-mail address from the mailing list.

MAILING LIST ADDRESSES

Each mailing list has two addresses. Make sure you send your messages to the appropriate address.

Mailing List Address

The mailing list address receives messages intended for the entire mailing list. This is the address you use to send messages you want all the people on the list to receive. Do not send subscription or unsubscription requests to the mailing list address.

Administrative Address

The administrative address receives messages dealing with administrative issues. This is the address you use to subscribe to or unsubscribe from a mailing list.

CHAPTER 13

NEWSGROUPS AND FTP

INTRODUCTION TO NEWSGROUPS

A newsgroup is a discussion group that allows people with common interests to communicate with each other.

There are thousands of newsgroups on every subject imaginable. Each newsgroup discusses a particular topic such as jobs offered, puzzles or medicine.

Usenet, short for Users' Network, refers to all the computers that distribute newsgroup information.

NEWSGROUP NAMES

The name of a newsgroup describes the type of information discussed in the newsgroup. A newsgroup name consists of two or more words, separated by periods (.).

The first word describes the main topic (example: rec for recreation). Each of the following words narrows the topic.

ARTICLES

A newsgroup can contain hundreds or thousands of articles.

Article

An article is a message that an individual posts, or sends, to a newsgroup. An article can be a few lines of text or the length of a small book.

I have a week's vacation coming up. Any suggestions for a fun place to spend it?

I had a great time in Hawaii.

I really enjoyed Mexico.

Get on a ship! A cruise is very relaxing!

Thread

A thread is an article and all replies to the article. A thread may include an initial question and the responses from other readers.

NEWSREADER

A newsreader is a program that lets you read and post articles to newsgroups.

Netscape Navigator comes with a built-in newsreader called Netscape News. Other popular newsreaders include News Xpress and Free Agent.

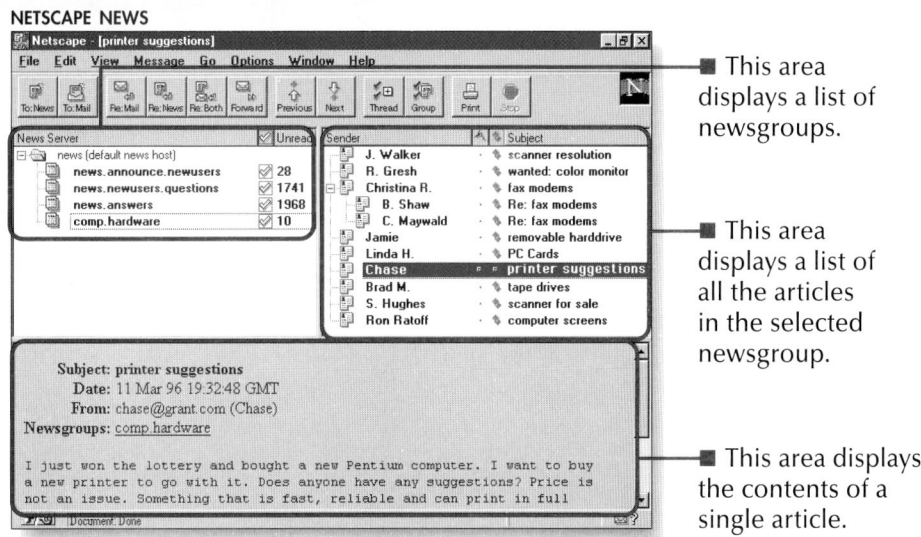

NETSCAPE NEWS

■ This area displays a list of newsgroups.

■ This area displays a list of all the articles in the selected newsgroup.

■ This area displays the contents of a single article.

SUBSCRIBE TO NEWSGROUPS

> You subscribe to a newsgroup you want to read on a regular basis.

If you no longer want to read the articles in a newsgroup, you can unsubscribe from the newsgroup at any time.

READ THE FAQ

The FAQ (Frequently Asked Questions) is a document that contains a list of questions and answers that often appear in a newsgroup.

The FAQ is designed to prevent new readers from asking questions that have already been asked. Make sure you read the FAQ before posting any articles to a newsgroup.

POST AN ARTICLE

You can post, or send, a new article to a newsgroup to ask a question or express an opinion. Thousands of people around the world may read an article you post.

MAIN NEWSGROUP CATEGORIES

alt (alternative)

General interest discussions that can include unusual or bizarre topics.

Examples include:

alt.fan.actors
alt.music.alternative

biz (business)

Business discussions that are usually more commercial than those in other newsgroups.

Examples include:

biz.books.technical
biz.jobs.offered

comp (computers)

Discussions of computer hardware, software and computer science.

Examples include:

comp.lang.pascal.borland
comp.security.misc

soc (social)

Discussions of social issues, including world cultures and political topics.

Examples include:

soc.college
soc.culture.caribbean

rec (recreation)

Discussions of recreational activities and hobbies.

Examples include:

rec.food.recipes
rec.skydiving

news

Discussions about newsgroups in general. Topics range from information about the newsgroup network to advice on how to use it.

Examples include:

news.admin.misc
news.announce.newgroups

INTRODUCTION TO FTP

File Transfer Protocol (FTP) lets you look through files stored on computers around the world and copy files that interest you.

FTP SITE

An FTP site is a place on the Internet that stores files. FTP sites are maintained by colleges, universities, government agencies, companies and individuals. There are thousands of FTP sites scattered across the Internet.

Private FTP Site

Some FTP sites are private and require you to enter a password before you can access any files.

Many corporations maintain private FTP sites to make files available to their employees and clients around the world.

Anonymous FTP Site

Many FTP sites are anonymous. Anonymous FTP sites let you access files without entering a password. These sites store huge collections of files that anyone can download, or copy, free of charge.

HOW FTP FILES ARE STORED

Files at FTP sites are stored in different directories.

manual.txt

porsche.gif

Just as folders organize documents in a filing cabinet, directories organize information at an FTP site.

■ **File Names**

Every file stored at an FTP site has a name and an extension, separated by a period. The name describes the contents of a file. The extension usually identifies the type of file.

THE FTP SCREEN

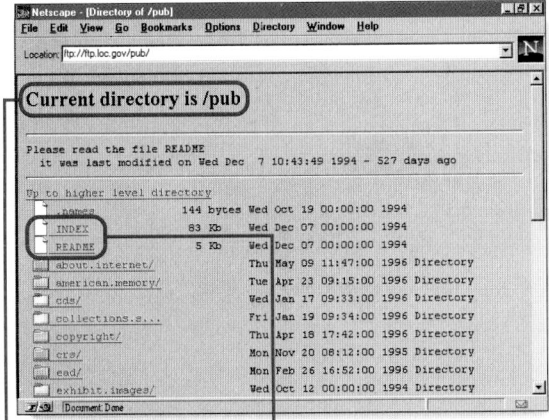

■ The files you want to copy to your computer are usually in the pub (public) directory.

■ Most well-established FTP sites include files that describe the rest of the files offered at the site. Look for files named "readme" or "index."

POPULAR FTP SITES

Some popular FTP sites include:

Library of Congress	ftp://ftp.loc.gov
Microsoft Corporation	ftp://ftp.microsoft.com
SunSITE	ftp://sunsite.unc.edu
Washington University	ftp://wuarchive.wustl.edu
Wiretap Library	ftp://wiretap.spies.com

The following Web site displays a large list of FTP sites:

http://hoohoo.ncsa.uiuc.edu/ftp-interface.html

There are many types of files available at an FTP site.

Text

You can get interesting documents for research and enjoyment, including books, journals, electronic magazines, computer manuals, government documents, news summaries and academic papers. Look for these extensions:

.asc   .doc   .htm   .html
.msg   .txt   .wpd

Sound

You can get theme songs, sound effects, clips of famous speeches and lines from television shows and movies. Look for these extensions:

.au   .ra   .ram   .snd
.wav

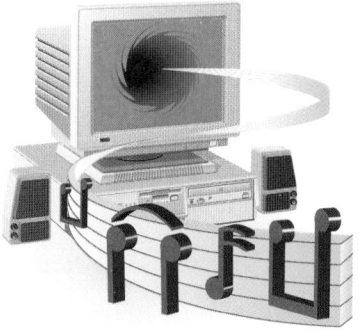

Graphics

You can get graphics such as computer-generated art, museum paintings and pictures of famous people. Look for these extensions:

.bmp   .eps   .gif   .jpg
.pict   .png

Video

You can get movie clips, cartoons, educational videos and computer-generated animation. Look for these extensions:

.avi   .mov   .mpg

Programs

You can get programs to use on your computer, such as word processors, spreadsheets, databases and games. Look for these extensions:

.bat   .com   .exe

SEARCH FOR FTP FILES

There are Web sites that let you search for files available at FTP sites around the world. This helps you find files of interest to you.

ARCHIE

Archie lets you search for specific files you have heard or read about. To use Archie, you need to know part of the name of the file you want to find.

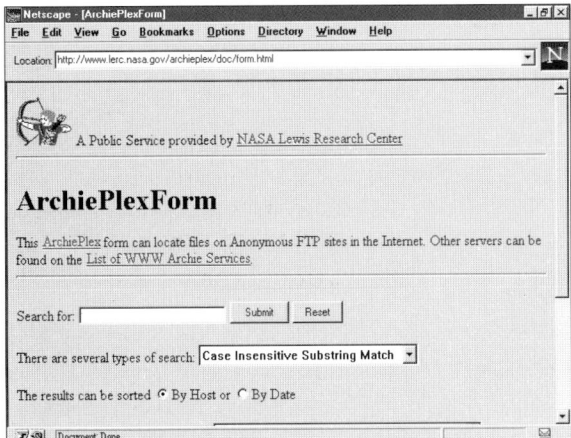

Archie is available at the following Web sites:

NASA
http://www.lerc.nasa.gov/archieplex

Rutgers University
http://www-ns.rutgers.edu/htbin/archie

SHAREWARE.COM

Shareware.com lets you search for specific files or browse through files stored at FTP sites around the world.

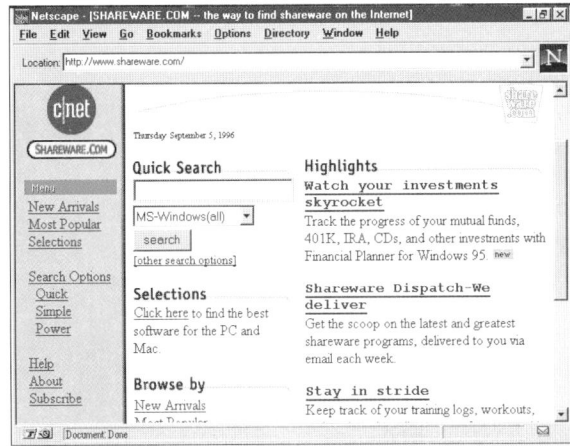

You can access shareware.com at the following Web site:

http://www.shareware.com

INDEX

A

abbreviation, e-mail, 201
access time, 74, 91
active matrix screen, 103
address
    e-mail, 199
    mailing list, 205
alias, Macintosh, 163
all-in-one case, 10, 152
Alt key, 22
animation on Web, 193
anonymous FTP site, 212
anti-virus program, 80
Apple desktop bus (ADB) port, Macintosh, 153
Apple key, 154
Apple menu, 163
application. *See also* program; software
    database, 128-131
    software, 2
        overview, 112-113
    spreadsheet, 120-127
    suite, 132-133
    word processor, 114-119
Archie, 215
arrow key, 23
article, newsgroup, 209, 210
asynchronous transfer mode (ATM) network, 173
audio/video port, Macintosh, 153
automated mailing list, 204
average access time
    CD-ROM drive, 91
    hard drive, 74

B

back up, 81, 83, 95, 96, 146
backbone, 183
backlight, 102
Backspace key, 23
battery, portable computer, 101
binary digit (bit), 5
bitmapped font, 34
bits per second (bps), 47
bookmark feature, Web browser, 191
browser, Web, 190-191
Bubble Jet printer, 28
buffer, print, 35
bundled software, 113
bus, 68-69, 158
byte, 5

C

cable, network, 169
cache
    disk, 77
    memory, 66-67
Caps Lock key, 22
card, expansion, 8, 14-15
cartridge, tape, 94, 97
case, computer, 7, 10, 152
CD-recordable (CD-R) drive, 93
CD-ROM, 86-93
    applications, 87
    disc, 86, 92
    drive, 4, 9, 86-91, 93
        alternatives, 93
        considerations when choosing, 90-91
        overview, 86
        portable computer, 106
    multimedia, 88-89
central processing unit. *See* CPU
characters per second (cps), 25
chart, overview, 127
client, 171
client/server network, 171
coaxial cable, 169
color
    depth, monitor, 43
    scanner, 56
COM port, 13
command, MS-DOS, 138
Command key, 154

PC Card, 108
PCMCIA Card and slot, 108
peer-to-peer network, 170
Pentium, 64
Pentium Pro, 64
peripheral, 2
peripheral component interconnect (PCI) bus, 69, 158
personal computer (PC), 6
pixel, 42
platform, 137
Plug and Play, 69, 145
plug-in, 192
pointing device, 18, 21
pointing stick, 104
port, 12-13, 153
port replicator, 109
portable, 10, 152. *See also* portable computer
portable computer, 100-109
 battery, 101
 CPU, 107
 docking station, 109
 infrared port, 109
 keyboard, 105
 Macintosh, 152
 memory, 107
 modem, 105
 overview, 100
 PCMCIA Card, 108
 pointing devices, 104
 port replicator, 109
 screen, 102-103
 sound card, 105
 speaker, 105
 storage devices, 106
PostScript, 32
power supply, 8, 11
PowerPC chip, 156
print
 buffer, 35
 spooler, 35
printer, 7, 24-35
 Bubble Jet, 28
 considerations when choosing, 24
 dot-matrix, 26-27
 dye sublimation, 33
 font, 34
 ink jet, 28-29
 laser, 30-32

 Macintosh, 154
 memory, 32
 multifunction laser, 31
 overview, 24-25
 resolution, 25
 solid ink, 33
 speed, 25
 thermal-wax, 33
printer control language (PCL), 32
private FTP site, 212
processing, 4
processor. *See* CPU
program. *See also* application; software
 anti-virus, 80
 application suite, 133
 as Internet feature, 180
 at FTP site, 214
 electronic mail, 198
 for connecting to Internet, 184
 icon, 141
 newsreader, 209
 overview, 112-113

Q

quarter-inch cartridge (QIC) drive, 97
query, 129
quoting, 202

R

random access memory (RAM). *See* memory
read-only memory (ROM), 61
reduced instruction set computer (RISC) chip, 156
refresh rate, monitor, 38
relational database, 131
removable hard drive, 76, 160
resident font, 34
resolution
 monitor, 42, 57
 printer, 25
 scanner, 57
router, 183

INDEX

terminal, 6
text
    at FTP site, 214
    in word processing document, 115, 116-117
    on Web, 192
thermal-wax printer, 33
thin-film transistor (TFT) screen, 103
thread, newsgroup, 209
tilt-and-swivel monitor base, 38
token-ring network, 173
touchpad, 21, 104
tower case, 10, 152
trackball, 21, 104
traffic, on network, 169
transmission control protocol/Internet protocol
    (TCP/IP), 182
Travan drive, 97
TrueType font, 34

U

UART chip, 46
uniform resource locator (URL), 189
uninterruptible power supply (UPS), 11
universal serial bus (USB), 13
unshielded twisted pair (UTP) cable, 169
upload, 183
Usenet, 208
user name, 199, 174
utilities, MS-DOS, 139

V

version, software, 113
VESA local bus (VL-Bus), 69
video
    at FTP site, 214
    on Web, 193
video card, 15
    Macintosh, 155
    memory, 41
    overview, 36
video graphics array (VGA) monitor, 43
video random access memory (VRAM), 41
videoconferencing, 168
virtual memory, 61
virtual reality modeling language (VRML), 193
virus, 80

W

W3. *See* Web
watts, 11
wavetable synthesis, 53
Web
    browser, 190-191
    home page, 190
    hypertext, 189
    hypertext transfer protocol (http), 189
    Java, 193
    multimedia, 192-193
    overview, 188-189
    page, 188
    search, 195
    security, 194
    shopping, 194
    site, 188
    3-D worlds, 193
    uniform resource locator (URL), 189
wide area network (WAN), 166
window RAM (WRAM), 41
Windows 3.1, 137, 140-143
Windows 95, 144-147
Windows for Workgroups 3.11 (WfWG), 143
Windows NT, 147
word processor, 114-119
World Wide Web. *See* Web
write-protect, floppy disk, 84
WWW. *See* Web

Z

zero insertion force (ZIF) socket, 65

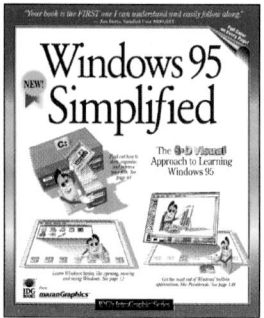

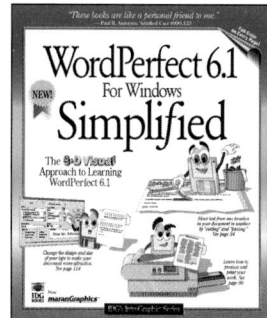
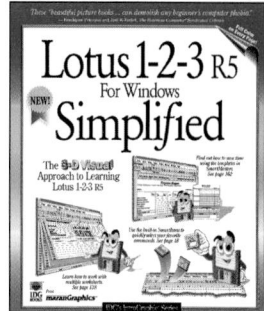

ORDER FORM

IDG BOOKS ®

TRADE & INDIVIDUAL ORDERS

Phone: **(800) 762-2974**
or **(317) 895-5200**
(8 a.m.–6 p.m., CST, weekdays)
FAX : **(317) 895-5298**

EDUCATIONAL ORDERS & DISCOUNTS

Phone: **(800) 434-2086**
(8:30 a.m.–5:00 p.m., CST, weekdays)
FAX : **(817) 251-8174**

CORPORATE ORDERS FOR 3-D VISUAL™ SERIES

Phone: **(800) 469-6616**
(8 a.m.–5 p.m., EST, weekdays)
FAX : **(905) 890-9434**

Qty	ISBN	Title	Price	Total

Shipping & Handling Charges

	Description	First book	Each add'l. book	Total
Domestic	Normal	$4.50	$1.50	$
	Two Day Air	$8.50	$2.50	$
	Overnight	$18.00	$3.00	$
International	Surface	$8.00	$8.00	$
	Airmail	$16.00	$16.00	$
	DHL Air	$17.00	$17.00	$

Subtotal _____

CA residents add applicable sales tax _____

IN, MA and MD residents add 5% sales tax _____

IL residents add 6.25% sales tax _____

RI residents add 7% sales tax _____

TX residents add 8.25% sales tax _____

Shipping _____

Total _____

Ship to:

Name _____

Address _____

Company _____

City/State/Zip _____

Daytime Phone _____

Payment: ☐ Check to IDG Books (US Funds Only)

☐ Visa   ☐ Mastercard   ☐ American Express

Card # _____ Exp. _____ Signature _____

maranGraphics™

IDG BOOKS WORLDWIDE REGISTRATION CARD

RETURN THIS REGISTRATION CARD FOR FREE CATALOG

Title of this book: Computers Simplified™, 3E

My overall rating of this book: ❑ Very good [1] ❑ Good [2] ❑ Satisfactory [3] ❑ Fair [4] ❑ Poor [5]

How I first heard about this book:

❑ Found in bookstore; name: [6] _____

❑ Advertisement: [8] _____

❑ Word of mouth; heard about book from friend, co-worker, etc.: [10] _____

❑ Book review: [7] _____

❑ Catalog: [9] _____

❑ Other: [11] _____

What I liked most about this book:

_____

_____

What I would change, add, delete, etc., in future editions of this book:

_____

_____

Other comments:

_____

Number of computer books I purchase in a year: ❑ 1 [12] ❑ 2-5 [13] ❑ 6-10 [14] ❑ More than 10 [15]

I would characterize my computer skills as: ❑ Beginner [16] ❑ Intermediate [17] ❑ Advanced [18] ❑ Professional [19]

I use ❑ DOS [20] ❑ Windows [21] ❑ OS/2 [22] ❑ Unix [23] ❑ Macintosh [24] ❑ Other: [25] _____
(please specify)

I would be interested in new books on the following subjects:
(please check all that apply, and use the spaces provided to identify specific software)

❑ Word processing: [26] _____

❑ Data bases: [28] _____

❑ File Utilities: [30] _____

❑ Networking: [32] _____

❑ Other: [34] _____

❑ Spreadsheets: [27] _____

❑ Desktop publishing: [29] _____

❑ Money management: [31] _____

❑ Programming languages: [33] _____

I use a PC at (please check all that apply): ❑ home [35] ❑ work [36] ❑ school [37] ❑ other: [38] _____

The disks I prefer to use are ❑ 5.25 [39] ❑ 3.5 [40] ❑ other: [41] _____

I have a CD ROM: ❑ yes [42] ❑ no [43]

I plan to buy or upgrade computer hardware this year: ❑ yes [44] ❑ no [45]

I plan to buy or upgrade computer software this year: ❑ yes [46] ❑ no [47]

Name: _____ Business title: [48] _____ Type of Business: [49] _____

Address (❑ home [50] ❑ work [51]/Company name: _____)

Street/Suite# _____

City [52]/State [53]/Zipcode [54]: _____ Country [55] _____

❑ **I liked this book!** You may quote me by name in future
IDG Books Worldwide promotional materials.

My daytime phone number is _____

IDG BOOKS

®

THE WORLD OF COMPUTER KNOWLEDGE

❑ YES!

Please keep me informed about IDG's World of Computer Knowledge.
Send me the latest IDG Books catalog.